1948, Elkhorn City Ball Park, Elkhorn City wins State Semi-Pro Title. Pictured are P. Musselman J. France, T. Deskins, B. Powe, T. Senters, J. Thornsberry, R. Picklesimer, J. Vance, B. Stumbo, F. Castle, J. Sullivan, C. Johnson, A. Train, J. Williamson, B. Venters and Fon "Ma" Mullins, Manager.

RUSSELL FORK RIVER BASIN AREA

PICTORIAL HISTORY

TURNER PUBLISHING COMPANY
Nashville, Tennessee

Dedicated to the Memory of
Jason Todd Rowe

Jason Todd Rowe, age 30 of Elkhorn City Kentucky. Born December 17, 1974, Died Thursday, December 23, 2004.

A tragic loss during the holiday for the City of Elkhorn City. Firefighters and the community of Elkhorn City are mourning the loss of one of their own. One who made a big difference in the community. Todd and other Elkhorn City Firefighters were conducting a training exercise at 7:45 P.M. EST using air lifting bags to raise the rear of the fire truck. While they were raising the truck, one of the bags shifted, came loose and propelled toward Todd. Todd was struck by the bag, killing him instantly.

He was employed by Kentucky Power Company and was Chief of the Elkhorn City Fire Department, a member of the National Rifle

Jason Todd Rowe

Association, an Eagle Scout, a member of El Hasa Shrine, a member of the Elkhorn City Voluntary Fire Department, a member of the Elkhorn City Ambulance Service, a Pike County Sheriff's deputy and a member of Jenkins Masonic Lodge #856. Todd served as public relations director of the Pike County Firefighters Association and a 911 Board Member.

During the funeral about twenty-four hundred people signed Todd's guest book. Funeral services were conducted at 1:00 P.M. Wednesday, December 29, 2004, at Elkhorn City Elementary School with about five hundred people in attendance. The procession to Wilson Cemetery was about five miles long, with about 80 fire trucks and other EMT vehicles.

The last call says it all...

GOOD BYE OUR TRUE AND DEAR FRIEND YOU WILL BE TRULY MISSED

Turner
PUBLISHING COMPANY

Turner Publishing Company Staff:
Keith Steele: Publishing Consultant
Charlotte Harris: Project Coordinator
Susan L. Harwood, Designer

Library of Congress Control No. 200414628

ISBN: 978-1-68162-546-1

Limited Edition

0 9 8 7 6 5 4 3 2 1

Contents

Preface 4

Buildings 5

Children 13

Churches and Baptisms 21

Couples 31

Dunleary 47

Events 49

Families 55

Groups 67

Industry 69

People 79

Police 101

Military 103

Modes of Transportation 115

Schools, Bands and Athletes 117

W.P.A. Projects 129

Memorial Pages 131

Index 143

Elkhorn City, Kentucky

Elkhorn City Area Heritage Council., Inc.
P.O.Box 1332
Elkhorn City, Ky, 41522

PREFACE

This undertaking of a pictorial history of the Elkhorn City Area and the Russell Fork River Basin is our first entrance into the many places and people that lived, loved and left their legacy along the crashing water of the Russell Fork of the Big Sandy. We have many pictures submitted by various people and we are indebted to them.

We know that we have not covered every occurrence in the area of the Russell Fork River Basin. Other works may cover areas and families we have not been able to cover in this book. However, we feel we have captured the essence of the Russell Fork and its communities.

In this book you will find the famous and the infamous, all contributing to the history we love so dearly and to our rich heritage.

Many people have contributed to this labor of love. We received more pictures than we placed in the book, but we will use them all in some way. We appreciate each and every picture and we will keep each one in our archives at the Heritage Council. Thanks go to the following members of the Elkhorn City Area Heritage Council, Inc. who have worked so diligently to bring us to our goal of finishing this book. Emalene Lee, Debbie Coleman, Neil Potter, Wendell Ward, Nick Marinaro, Nina Aragon and Patricia Belcher and all the others who helped in any way, especially those who brought pictures.

We also appreciate the patience you have shown us with the delays in preparation. We did not realize the amount of work involved. We thank everyone who purchased a book and we know you will enjoy it and learn more of our rich heritage and history.

Thanks to all,

Timothy D. Belcher
President, ECAHC, Inc.

Board of Directors of ECAHC, Inc
Patricia Belcher
Nick Marinaro
Neil Potter
Rodney Potter
Jim Stapleton
Peggy Sykes
Wendell Ward

Officers of ECAHC, Inc.
Tim Belcher, President
Nina Aragon, Vice President
Renee Kendrick, 2nd Vice President
Debbie Coleman, Secretary
Terry Thompson, Treasurer

Buildings

Jackson's Merchantile in Elkhorn City, Kentucky, about 1952. Marty Jackson in front.

Above: This cabin is located at Rock Lick Creek-Big Rock, Virginia, in Buchanan County. Built in the late 1800's. Said to have been built by John Wess Lee who was married to Mary (Polly) Elswick. John Wess Lee is the grandfather of Emalene Lee who submitted this picture. She has reason to believe that her dad Willie (Bill) Lee was born in this cabin. It is still standing as of April 2004.

Right: Elkhorn City Depot Elkhorn City, Kentucky. Circa 1930s

Right: Ray Jackson, Doug Jackson on Pine Street, Elkhorn City, Kentucky.

Below: Wintery scene on Pine Street, Elkhorn City, Kentucky.

Above: This photo taken by E.C. Blair of the first house in Elkhorn City. It was owned by William Ramey and was located directly across from the present day school buildings. E.C. Blair was employed by the railroad and worked in the (Eastend) of Elkhorn City before marrying Gaynelle Looney. He was known to have taken many pictures in the area.

Left: Leslie Seaton Anderson and Dennis Gene Anderson in front of Cumberland Confectionary on Main Street, Elkhorn City, Kentucky. 1945

Right: Elswick Hotel, Main Street, Elkhorn City, Kentucky.

Left: Old Hospital, was located on Main Street behind the present location of Justice Dental Office.

Sykes Whiskey Store and old Texaco Garage on Elkhorn Street, Elkhorn City, Kentucky.

Above: Log Sweeney standing on Main Street, in the background is the Old Bank Building.

Right: John Hackney Store and Home on Russell Street in Elkhorn City. 1940

Left: Mason and Clara Holley Ramey's log cabin(home) located on Little Beaver Creek near Elkhorn City, Kentucky.

Right: Elswick Store on Elkhorn Street Elkhorn City, Kentucky. There is a Dollar General Store where this store was.

Right: The Drummer House left to right Roy Looney, Gay Looney, Louemma Looney Mullins and Mae Marrs.

Left: THE ROCK BUILDING Located just north of Elkhorn City.

Elkhorn Theatre Elkhorn City, Kentucky. LaVern Belcher Ratliff (girl)

The first Theatre in Elkhorn City was called the MURPHY Theatre built in 1939 by Autie Jackson. It was located on Main Street in Elkhorn City.

Main Street 1922 Frede Canada Sanders building where the new library stands now. Located on Main Street.

Kelly Marinaro Building pictured left to right Cataldo (Kelly), Maria and Mary (daughter) Marinaro. Located on Pine Street in Elkhorn City, Kentucky.

Wig Ratliff building on Russell Street, Elkhorn City, Kentucky.

Home of Will and Jenny Ward. 1930

Edgewater Mining Camp Hellier, Kentucky.

Left: George Stewart Jr. Standing, second girl from left sitting is Roberta Potter. Teen Age - Hi Jinx owned by George Stewart Jr. was at Pool Point Curve.

1983 or 1984, train derailment, East Elkhorn Street, Trails End Restaurant and formerly Dr. Odom's Clinic.

A.F. Amburgey Store on Russell Street in Elkhorn City, Kentucky.

Marion Daniel Ramey last home place Head of left fork of Big Card Creek Mouth Card, Kentucky. Built early 1900's probably 1904 or 1905. Picture taken in early 1950s.

Old City Hall at Hellier, Kentucky.

Left: Hellier Café (later Hellier Post Office) in 1920

The Reece Home Place. 1942

Mrs. Miles home in Draffin, Kentucky.

Right: Home of Grant and Harriet Hawkins thought to be located on Pond Creek road at Draffin, Kentucky.

Children

Left: Left to right: Virgie Rakes, Della Bennette, Lauria Sanders, Otto Sykes, Virgil Sykes and Acy Sykes. May 1916

Above: Back row left to right: Chester, John, Junior and Ray. Second row: Ellis and Ira Potter. Front row: Mary and Worth Clevinger.

Left: Jack Tackett son of Jeff Davis Tackett and Cordia Childres Tackett

Left: Leslie Seaton Anderson and Dog on Main Street, Elkhorn City, Kentucky.

Below: Left to right: Mirul Powel, Clyde Mullins and Burgess "Shiloh" Slone near Bowen's Rock. 1923

Above: Eliza Hawkins Keeton and Alva Hawkins Childers, children of Grant and Harrett Mays Hawkins.

Right: Berta and Flossie Kendrick, Wolfpit Mining Houses. 1924

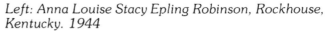

Left: Anna Louise Stacy Epling Robinson, Rockhouse, Kentucky. 1944

Below: Evelyn, Archie, Sam and Emma Childers, children of Lawrence and Alva Childers.

Above: This photo of Carmen Sanders and her brothers, Bob and Harold Butler, was taken in 1913 in Pike County, Kentucky. It was turned into a postcard later, which was sent to Mrs. Sarah Butler by her son, Richard, in Van Lear, Kentucky. The cost of the postage was one cent.

Left: Rodney Benton (left) and Ferdie Canada Sanders (right), Elkhorn Street, Elkhorn City, KY.

At left: Left to right: Betty Wright, Sue Mullins and Sondra Wright, Elkhorn City, Bridge Sreet, about 1945.

Below: Twins Alvin and Alva Hawkins, born July 13, 1907.

Above: 3 boys in front row left to right: Dave Ratliff, Burnie Ratliff and Glen Ratliff.

Right: Helen Tackett and Ten, her dog Elkhorn Street, Elkhorn City.

Left: Louisa Maynor (with black skirt), Nora (Maynor) Stapleton age 2 or 3 (standing in chair) and Gracie (Ratliff) Williams (one with hat), Elkhorn City about 1914.

Above: Left to right: John Robert Johnson, Helen Lee and Sandy Ratliff in their Easter Clothes in 1956.

Right: Children of Mason and Clara Ramey at home on Little Beaver Creek, Elkhorn City, Kentucky. Left to right: Peggy, Bobby Mason holding Vena, about 1941.

Left: Helen Louise Lee standing on foot bridge leading to her home on the hill at Pond Creek, Draffin.

Below: Boy Scouts leading parade in Elkhorn City about 1976.

Above: Children of Carmen and Edna Ramey, right fork of Beaver Creek. Great, great, great grandchildren of William Ramey. 1955

Right: Patty Caudill (left) and Nancy Ward (right)... Nancy Ward fell off tricycle and died... after which it is said she played in the mansion that Richard "Hank" Salyer lives in today.

Right: Laythe E. Sykes and Eddie Earl Slone, 1948.

Below: Right to left: Tolbert Lexter Cantrell, Edward Cantrell, Allen Cantrell and Curtis Cantrell taken in 1910 or 1911.

Above: Left to right: Chloa Ramey Bartley, Myrtle Ramey and Clint Ratliff, about 1916.

Left: Eizabeth Akers Elliott (left) and Nancy Akers Farmer (right)

Left to right: Eugene Barke and Reid Wallace

Children of Mose and Cora (Hunt) Potter. Left to right: Edna, Kelsa, Rans (baby) and Verta.

Joyce Loar and Juanita Wilburn, Elkhorn Street 1938. Building in background is Jackson Wholesale that burned around 1940.

Lila Lee Ratliff in back of Frank Wallace house.

TWO GOOD FARMERS... R.G. (Worm) Wallace and Morris Wallace. 1942

Churches and Baptisms

Above: Grapevine Church of Christ Youth Group, Back row: 2nd from left Florence Adkins Ramey, Carolina Blackburn Adkins, Nerva Thompson Adams.

Right: Doris Lipps and Grace Holmes, missionaries from Alliance Church, visited schools in Elkhorn City area during the years 1940s through the 1950s and taught the bible to the students.

An Old time Baptizing probably in th early 1900s, somewhere on the shores of the Big Sandy River.

Left: Lee and Bertha Swiney Adams being baptized near mouth of Kettle Camp. Isaac Sanders, Minister Sweet Home Regular Baptist Church in Elkhorn Creek. May 1969

Right: Established in 1856, Cedar Grove Church, Old Regular Baptists, Beaver Creek

Corner Stone laying for the Methodist Church. 1909

Right: Ground breaking for the Elkhorn City Baptist Church. (Circa 1950) Homer Stone, Tom Self, Bart Bingham, Evelyn Johnson, Virginia Wright, Vicars Slone, Clyde Beavers, Ruth Coleman, J.D. Wright, Walter Coleman, Jerry Bailiff, David Thomas Johnson.

Mildred Weigel and Clara Eicher came to Draffin, KY in 1940. They held Sunday School in the community using the Lower and Upper Pond School houses until a church was built. They also held a chapel service in both schools on Friday, teaching bible stories and Bible verses to the children. They also taught Sunday School and Bible stories at Belcher School. Only time and eternity will reveal the effects of their ministry in Draffin and surrounding areas.

Left: Mildred Weigel (left) and Clara Eicher (right). These two Missionary ladies came to the Draffin area over 60 years ago.

Left: Draffin Christian & Missionary Alliance Church built in 1960. A vision of two Missionary Ladies, Miss Mildred Weigel and Miss Clara Eicher. In September 1998, this church congregation merged with The Community Alliance Church located at Regina, Kentucky.

Rigth: Hellier Sunday School, September 10, 1911

Salute to the Elkhorn City Church of Christ Christian

Present Day

Above: 1931

Below: Early 1940s

Above: 1957 or 1958

Left: 1970

Prior to the year 1923, Mrs. Lillie Deskins, Mrs. Alpha Anderson, Mrs. Stella Ratliff, Ma Swiney, Mrs. Mellie Hackney and Kate Cross Good were the first Christians desiring to establish a New Testament Church in Elkhorn City.

In 1924 following a tent revival the church was partly organized. Regular meetings were held in the old theater on Russell Street. Florence Spradlin and Merta Smith were baptized at this revival. Near the end of 1924 they moved to a little school house on 5th Street. In 1929, James Hatcher, owner of

Leslie Anderson, Greeter – 1992. Nick Kendrick coming in door.

Hatcher Hotel in Pikeville, made a donation of a lot and Mr. Ballad Weddington, a Pikeville businessman gave the $100.00 for the building fund. Henry and George Thompson, Mont Coleman, Joe Ratliff, Perry Anderson, John Spradlin and Basil Swiney began laying the foundation.

Evangelists, Henry Thompson, H.G. Thompson, J.W. West, G.C. Clark and many others got the work started. Many times the women had to serve communion aided by youth, Sadie Anderson and Mary Jo Ratliff. Even so no Lords Day ever passed in the history of Church at the Elkhorn City, that the Lord's Supper has not been served.

First Elders were John Spivey, H.H. Thompson, George Hunt, Joe Ratliff.

Deacons: F.F. Maynor, S.K. Flanary, Ira Deskins, Bart Rowe.

Laymen filling the pulpit in the early years were Charley Ramey, Clarence Burke and Pete Spradlin. Calvin Mullins was also a good helper and many other women joined the work, Mrs. Bill England, Mrs. Alice Elswick, Mrs. Willie Salyer, Mrs. John Spivey, Mrs. Fonnie Maynor, Mrs. Lloyd Wright among others.

The first minister was called in April 1933, Harold Sanstrom came to stay for 3 months and stayed 2 years, his pay was $20.00 a month.

During this time Julian Hunt, Kenis Hunt, Alvis Ford, Alex Hunt and Bennie Hunt held revivals. In 1942 Brother H.J. Farmer and Lula Farmer came as full time servants. Parsonage and classrooms were added during Brother Farmers' term and was named Farmer Fellowship Hall.

On November 1945 the following members organized and adopted the Articles of Incorporation which was certified by Perry Anderson, H.J. Farmer, W.H. Adkins, Basil Swiney, Mrs. Alpha Sword, Mrs. Stella Ratliff, W.C. Burke, Mrs. Edna Senter, Mrs. Cretia Mullins and Mrs. John Spradlin. The name of the Corporation shall be Church of Christ (Christian) Elkhorn City, Kentucky, Post Office, Praise, Kentucky.

In 1951, Joseph Bachman Jr., held a two week revival which resulted in 77 additions. Both the church and Bible School attendance began to grow .

Sunday School Superintendent and Elder Herbert Gibson was tragically killed in auto accident on July 14, 1954 and after his death a new class was organized to honor his hard work and dedication, the Gibson Fellowship Class. Attendance records were broken in 1951 and again in 1955. In 1951 the attendance record was symbolically broken by Herbert Gibson and again in 1955 by Herbert's son Mack Gibson.

A baptistery was purchased and installed by Thurman Elswick. Previously we held baptisms at the creek or river.

Some of our great teachers have been Alpha Anderson, Oma Powell, Catherine Anderson, Eugene Sanders, Betty Sanders, Geraldine Francisco, Emil Francisco, Faye Belcher, J.D. Wright, Imal Kendrick, Jean Prater, Edna Senter, Leslie Anderson, Nick Kendrick, Lorene Salyer, Goffery Salyer, Ralph Ramey, Bessie Ramey, Elster Robinson, David Sanders, Richard Elswick, Barry Potter and Roger Lee.

Our ministers have been, H.J. Farmer, Thomas McFadden, Julian Hunt, Robert Allison, Tom Neff, Morris Mounts, Coleman Roach, Earl Stiff, E.W. Damron, Roy Robinson, Fred Balding, David Bolton, Harold Hamm, Tim McIntosh, Bill Ford and Jim Edd Belcher, present minister.

Our present building was started in 1967 with a $1,000.00 donation from Lynn Anderson Brown. It was completed in 1968. The first baptism was Leslie Seaton Anderson in February 1968. Our minister at that time when our present building was finished was David Bolton, he left for a short time and came back in the early 1980s and preached until his death in May of 1985.

We have been blessed to have had many fine Christian men in the leadership of our church. Bruce Prater, J.D. Wright, Ralph Ramey, Arnold Epling, Mason Ramey, Doug Robinson, Leslie Anderson, Otis Elswick, C.R. Anderson, Lundy Elswick, Ray Ratliff, Elster Robinson, Richard Elswick, Howard Bird, Everett Senter, Frank Salyer Jr., George Mullins and Elmer Kendrick.

Also many other of our Saints have gone home: Aunt Ida Wright, Alpha Anderson, Rushie Puckett, Stella Ratliff, Violet Elswick, Mary Elswick, Chester Elswick, Pebble Elswick, Margaret Elswick, Russell and Thelma Wiley, Cowan Ratliff, Maxie Stiltner, Margie Self, Sadie Belcher, Lorene Salyer, Bessie Ramey, Clara Ramey, Debbie Ford.

In 1980, Leslie Anderson started our greeters program, Leslie greeted every one with a smile and a hug and this continues today with two greeters each Sunday.

Present Elders: Roger Lee, Chairman of the Board, Goffery Salyer, David Sanders, Steve Taylor, Sammie Rose, Nick Kendrick, Foster Wallace, Brock Anderson and Mike Honaker.

Deacons: Victor Fields, Tony Cantrell, David Compton, George Anderson, Henry Anderson, Benny Ramey, Mack Gibson, Sammy Belcher, Tommy Rowe and Grondall Potter II.

Trustees: Goffery Salyer, David Sanders, Mack Gibson, Victor Fields and Mike Honaker.

The Elkhorn City Church of Christ was started by a group of Christian ladies who met in their homes for Bible Study, Prayer Meetings and Circle Meetings. The Women's Christian Union has continued this tradition with being very involved with the work of the Church. Women have had a vital part from the beginning to this day.

The seed in the beginning which was the least of all seeds began to shoot forth its buds in tender hope.

This page Compliments of Lois Cantrell

Elkhorn City Baptist Church

First Building - 1921

The Elkhorn City Baptist Church was built on the prayers, faith and sacrifices of a few dedicated Christmas in the Elkhorn City area. Jemimah Meade and her daughter Katherine Meade, now deceased, realized the need and began writing letters to other Christians in the area asking them to pray for a church. G.T. Hinton and a representative of the State Board came to visit her. In 1920 a small group of people began having services in the old store building belonging to John Hackney. Soon after this the church was organized.

There were eleven charter members. They were Mr. and Mrs. G.T. Hinton, Mr. and Mrs. Fred Menefee, Mrs. J.D. Meade, Katherine Meade, Charles Meade, Mrs. Pinson, Mr. and Mrs. R.C. Simpson and Ed Elliot. It is believed that the church was organized in 1920 and the building was completed in 1921. Two ladies who made a great impact on the beginning of this church were Beulah Gaines and Miss Trabue, sent by the State Board.

The first record of deacons was Willie Belcher and Johnson Nave. Many others followed. Miss Annie Allen came to Elkhorn City as a missionary and a mission was started at Dunleary. Brother Ferris was the pastor and after a short time he and his son drowned in Russell Fork River, behind Elkhorn Street.

Nell Tackett Elswick became a member of this church in 1925. She is the old-est member in the service of the church. Space is not available to tell of all her contributions and services to the church. She has been pianist and organist of the church since 1936, and is still the teacher of the "Bethany" class.

This church had a spirit for missions at an early date. The first mission was started at Wolfpit, then Hellier. The Marrowbone Baptist Church was established in 1942 from Hellier Mission. Faith Baptist Church at Jimmie's Creek was an end result of the Yellow Hill Mission.

Brother A.O. Allison served as pastor for 11 years. Much can be said of the many accomplishments that came about during his pastorate. The ground work for the new building started while he was pastor.

One of the greatest spiritual revivals in the history of the church was held by Doyle Denny, in 1955. There were 27 professions of faith, two joined by letter and one by statement. The baptismal service was held behind the school building. During his pastorate of 2 years, there were 117 members added to the roll. The Brotherhood was organized at this time.

Elkhorn City Baptist Church – Second building dedicated July 1957

In 1956, the church bought the property to build a new church. The ground breaking was held April 2, 1956 and on July 7, 1957, the first services were held in the new church and the dedication was July 14, 1957.

The Fellowship Hall was dedicated on December 12, 1962. The church has participated in several World Mission Conferences, World Changers, Cooperative Program, Pike Association of Baptists and Elkhorn City Ministerial Association.

Another dream was fulfilled when the church under the leadership of Brother Cleon Webb, provided a comfortable pastorium for the pastor and his family. It was dedicated in 1970.

There has been an ongoing schedule of activities at the Mt. View Nursing Home. These activities include: Bible study, bingo and an educational program taught by retired teachers.

New addition dedicated Oct. 26, 2003

A library was started with Jenny Salyer as director. Most of the library has been provided through memorial gifts or donated materials by friends and members.

The WMU has had a great part in keeping missions alive in the church. Much credit is due to the great leadership of Nell Elswick.

During WWII a young member of the church, Paul Owens, was called to be with the Lord while serving his country.

In 1977 the church placed a time capsule containing a variety of church records in the cornerstone and this was opened in 2000.

Brother David Peters became pastor of the ECBC in February 2000. He and his young family brought new energy to the church. Many ministries were started that attracted several new, young families. AWANA, a ministry program for children through teens, was organized and grew to over 75 children and 30 adult teachers. This increased our Sunday School enrollment.

This growth created an acute need for expansion of the church campus.

A Vision Committee was formed in the fall of 2000 to seek God's will for the addition of classrooms and a fellowship hall. On April 28, 2001, the church signed a contract with Summit Engineering to develop 13 new classrooms, a pastor's office, administrative offices, two bathrooms, a new kitchen and a HVAC system for the entire church and a large fellowship hall.

The Sulphur Fork Baptist Builders came to Elkhorn City on June 6, 2002, and with much hard work, prayer and praising, the building was under roof within a week. God proved once again to be faithful and true. The addition was completed within the $300,000 budgeted debt. The new addition was dedicated October 26, 2003 with Bro. David Peters presiding.

There is not enough space to name all the members, pastors, deacons, teachers and persons who deserve to be mentioned for their Christian services—but there was Roy Looney. He served the church faithfully for the 37 years he was a member. He loved hauling in the children and getting one of the men to go visiting with him. He was called "Candy Man" at the nursing home.

To all the past and present members of the Elkhorn City Baptist Church—May you always be about your Father's business, winning souls for Christ and building up His kingdom.

Elkhorn City United Methodist Church

*United Methodist Church
Yesterday*

*Dora Briggs, Established Methodist
Church – 1910*

*United Methodist Church
Today*

In 1902 Rev. J.M. Ackman, District Superintendent of the Ashland District first visited Elkhorn City. The population was 160. He found some Methodist living here who showed enough interest to acquire two lots on Main Street. The church failed to be built on them so these lots were deeded back to Elkhorn City Land and Improvement.

In the early months of 1908, Reverend Ackman sent the following missionaries to Elkhorn City for the purpose of establishing a Methodist Church. Miss Dora Bridges, Miss Margaret Globe and Miss Snyder as deaconesses. Miss Bridges was born and raised in Loveland, New Jersey in 1880. She was 28 years old. The ladies began working and soon began having Sunday School and Church services in a school building situated next door to the present church. Many of the members urged her to begin raising money to build a new church. There were no organized churches in Elkhorn City at this time.

First Subscription List
Methodist Episcopal Church of Elkhorn City,
Kentucky, Pike County

We, the undersigned members and friends of the Methodist Episcopal Church of Elkhorn City, Pike County, Kentucky, do in view of the fact that this community needed a church, and also has seen fit to come into the community, and by their efforts erect a church to this said denomination, do hereby subscribe opposite our names, the amount we are willing to pay to assist in the construction of said church.

Witness our signatures, this day of May 1908. J.B. Polley $25.00, A. Keathly $5.00, Roland Elswick $5.00, J.H. Hutchings $5.00, Dr. R.C. Booth, $5.00, L.D. Polley, $5.00, Mrs. V.A. Stockard, $5.00, Rev. J.M. Ackman, $25.00, Miss Dora Bridges, $17.50, Mrs. Orville Cure, $8.25, and Mrs. J.B. Ramey $15.00, Total $117.00.

In 1908 a lot was bought on Aug. 30, 1909 from the Elkhorn Land and Improvement Company. Parties of the first part to L.R. Thornsberry, Dora Bridges, Lewis Clevinger, G. Beldon Long, L.D. Polley, trustees of the Methodist Episcopal Church.

By April 23, 1910 the building was almost completed. The building was built by J.H. Honaker from Pikeville, Kentucky. Dedication was June 21, 1910. A special train ran from Ashland bringing members of the choir of the First Methodist Church. Since the railroad bridge had not been built, the visitors crossed the river by boat. Reverend Ackman presided at the dedication.

Miss Bridges continued to serve as pastor until 1912. She died in August 1948 in Bloomington, Kentucky. After building a small orphanage for children.

Until 1947 the pastors and family had their parsonage in the rooms in back of the church. On July 25, 1947, we received a deed for a house and lot on Main Street for our parsonage. Katherine Meade and R.B. Hollar were former owners. Trustees were Donald Elswick, A.A. Ratliff, and John F. Ford.

By 1960 our membership had become so large we needed Sunday School classes. After much planning we were able on October 9, 1961 to have a ground breaking for a new Educational Building. Dedication of the building that year was by Reverend Leroy Sanders and Russel R. Palton, District Superintendent.

In 1973 to 1979 our pastor was A.A. Frederick. Under his leadership we were able to enlarge our sanctuary, install new windows and brick our building.

The Elkhorn City United Methodist Church had our Centennial Celebration on August 31, 2002. This was a special day when our church family who had moved away joined us in remembrance, songs, dinner and prayer.

Through prayers and dedication and many pastors, people have been led to know our Savior, Jesus Christ.

Jerry D. Hall, Pastor
Hester P. Hunt, Church Historian

Couples

Left: Jess and Polly Fields Bartley, Married April 23, 1868.

Below: Margaret Briggs and Jimmie Coleman, Main Street, Elkhorn City

Left: George and Mary Potter Ramey, Right fork of Beaver Creek, Kentucky. Early 1959.

Left: H.G. and Annie Crowder Belcher

Below: Mason and Clara Holley Ramey at her parents yard on 5th Street. The Community church located in background is where the Elkhorn City Church of Christ (Christian) held services before building in 1930s. It was also used as school.

Above: Autie D. and Missouri Jackson on Elkhorn Street, Elkhorn City, about 1928 or 1929.

Right: Guy and Florence Potter, early 1950s

Right: Harriett and Grant Hawkins

Below: Lon and Flossie Rowe, owners of Rowe Grocery, Harless Creek.

Above: Sophia and Nevada Kendrick (died in 1927) Wolfpit, Kentucky. 1910

Left: Roy and Melvina Ward, Road Creek, Kentucky, May 10, 1917.

Right: Earl and Verna Gibson Stacy, Pond Creek, Draffin, Kentucky. In the 1940s

Katherine Coleman Mullins and Arthur "Mock" Mullins, Elkhorn City, Kentucky. 1955

Wilson and Ivil Spears

Left: Harve and Alice Maynor Stacy

Flem and Josie Castle

Carmen and Edna Ramey of Little Beaver Creek taken at Conaway, Virginia, November 21, 1945.

Right: Bill and Elizabeth Senter Reece

Below: Malinda "Lindy" Potter and James Sweeney (or Swiney)

Above: Lill Vanover and Ray Potter

Right: Walter and Lydia O'Quinn Breeding, Conaway Creek, Buchanan County, Virginia. 1946

Left: Clarence and Anna Stewart, June 18, 1932. Picture made at present day Clinchfield Overlook. The first vehicle ever that far down the Mountain.

Above: Riley and Winnie Belcher

Left: Dr. Sanders and Vergie Maynard, Marrowbone Drive, about 1920.

Right: Jessie and Ann Stacy

Above: Percy and Alma Potter, 1956

Right: Bev Wallace (baby), James Franklin and Elizabeth Mullins Wallace, Elkhorn City, Kentucky. 1888

Left: William Bill and Mary Vance Coleman

Above: Sarah Beth Coleman and S.W. "Uncle Buck" Coleman at Wolfpit, Kentucky. 1920

Left: Edward and Lucretia Mullins Ramey, Henry Clay, Kentucky. 1920

Right: Isom and Cosby Bentley Senter. Isom was the son of Hulda Mullins and Stephen Henry Senter. Cosby was the daughter of Eliza Moore and James Bentley.

Below: Susellen Sanders and John Boone Potter

Above: Log Sweeney and Sue Kendrick Sweeney

Right: J.P. and Emily Agnes Spradlin at Breaks Interstate Park.

Left: Stewart and Elza May Lee at their home on Pond Creek, Draffin, Kentucky. In the early 1960s

Above: John Morgan and Spicy Damron Potter

Left: Jean Gray Hall and Paul Stiltner, Elkhorn Creek, Kentucky. 1950s

Right: Hulda Church Belcher and Basil Belcher, Mouthcard, Kentucky.

Above: Harold C. and Creattia Butler

Right: Suzie Caroline Gunnells Davis and Albert Archie Davis, about 1940

Left: Mr. and Mrs. Frank Loar

Below: Alfred Mays and Harriet Mays Hawkins, Elkhorn City, Kentucky. 1960s

Above: W.S. and Amanda Akers

Left: Hawkins and Louisa Childers Ratliff

Palmer and Josie Belle Little Childers. 1950s

Bob and Nancy Akers Farmer

Above: Amos Nelson Watson and Lola Isabelle Freeman Watson on their wedding day. Picture take late 1800s.

Left: David Crockett Sifers and Ollie Smith on their wedding day, January 10, 1912. They are the grandparents of Janice Cook of Elkhorn City, Kentucky.

Left: Lillie May Potter Hawkins and Fronzo Sturgell, Wedding Picture, May 20, 1929

Below: Myrtie Belcher Chaney and Jefferson Chaney

Alice Belcher Salyer and Frank Salyer, Little Beaver Creek.

Will and Jenny Ward. Jenny was a midwife.

Right: John Wess and Mary Polly Elswick Lee. John Wess was the son of Richard and Nancy Fuller Lee. Mary "Polly" was the daughter of Henderson and Catherine Looney Elswick.

Left: Willie B. and Evelyn May standing by the taxi cab.

Dunleary

Right: Corbin Spears, Dunleary, Kentucky

Below: Dunleary Company Street, left to right: Tom Johnson, unidentified, Perry Anderson, Leslie J. Anderson and H. Hatfield. 1939

Above: Dunleary Mining Camp during the 1930s

Left: Dunleary Ferry, 1939

Right: Dunleary Store about 1915

Above: Children of Lula Spears at Dunleary, Kentucky.

Right: Dunleary, Kentucky Baseball Team, 1919 or 1920

Ferry Boat, Dunleary, Kentucky. 1940

Events

Left: Train Wreck on Elkhorn Street, 1983 or 1984

Above: Mayor J.D. Wright and Goebel Newsom presenting G.T. Hawkins the key to Elkhorn City. Left to right: J.D. Wright, G. Tom Hawkins and Goebel Newsom.

Left: Early 1940s Scrap Iron Collection Parade, on what is now Patty Lovelass Drive. Former R.T. Elswick store on left.

Right: 1909 Baseball Team. Standing left to right: Floyd Castle, Ellison Bickford, Oral Bickford, Elmer Alloway and Cleve Wallace. Stitting: Charlie Wallace, ____ Billiter, K. Hubbard, Charles Bickford and Oral Wallace. Boy in front is Ozal Wallace.

Making Molasses – extracting juice from sugar cane.

Molasses being boiled in evaporator pans.

Above: Scrape Iron Drive during WWII Elkhorn City, 1940 to 1944.

Right: Louisa Ratliff standing on dam that fed water into fish ponds, around 1950.

Left: Homes that were in the flood area of the 1957 flood at Pond Bottom, Draffin, Kentucky.

Above: Alva Childers making apple pies. Alva was Pike County Mother of the Year in 1990s.

Left: Vern Bickford – Pro Baseball Card. From Hellier, KY and played for the Braves.

Right: Clyde Mullins at Elkhorn City Cemetery.

Below: 1940s TRAIN DEPOT

Above: Elkhorn Street left to right: Otto Sykes, Laythe Sykes and Mert Williams. 1949 Hog Killing Time.

Left: Donald Elswick at Memorial Service at Elkhorn City Cemetery

Left: Elkhorn City Band

Above: Ma Ramey spinning wool for clothes for her family.

Left: Ruth Belcher drawing water for chickens, 1930.

Letcher County, Kentucky. Funeral and burial of Devil John Wright. 1931 (Submitted by Bill Gibson)

The funeral of Bart Rowe, Elkhorn City's only Town Marshall that was killed in the line of duty. Early 1920s.

Families

Left: "Ma" Ramey standing in front of Grandpa H. Belcher's store with Shug, Herman and Hersel Salyer. Seated are Clifford Salyer, Ralph and Eleanor Belcher

Below: Left to right: Elsie Belcher, Lessie Hylton, Chester Belcher, Emelene Belcher, Basil Belcher and Lula Branham. 1920s

Right: Levisa Fork, Elaine Scott 2nd from right.

Right: Children and grandchildren of Isom and Cosby Bentley Senter in the early 1900s. Front row left to right: Everett Senter, Golda Meadows, Opal Senter, Ruth Belcher, Georgia Senter and Elmer Belcher. Second row left to right: Minerva Senter, Jennie Senter, Eliza Senter, Pearl Senter and Grace Belcher.

Hackney Family – left to right: Otis, William, Mellie, Florida. Front row: Roma and Eunice., 5th Street, Elkhorn City, Kentucky. 1916

Mont Coleman and daughter Bessie Coleman in 1950s.

Right: Lois Slone Ramey (on porch), John Hackney (carrying wood) and Bennie Slone (child), Beaver Bottom, 1943

Left: Left to right: Lorene, Reed, John Morgan Potter, Curt and Maxie Salyers, Spicy Potter, Oscar and Mae Epling, Allison and Katie Deskins Potter. Elkhorn Creek, Ashcamp, Kentucky, 1950s.

William Belcher, Maggie Crowder Belcher, Ralph Belcher, Billy Belcher and Eleanora Belcher. 1950

Left to right: Bud Hopkins (on horse), Harrison Thacker and Burtha Thacker (last lady standing far right).

Left: George and Clarinda Colley Potter Family — First row: George and Clarinda Potter Second row: Betty, Richard, James H., Alex, Adam and James Potter. Elkhorn City, Kentucky. Circa 1914

Right: Grant Hawkins and Daniel Childers, grandson. 1940

Below: Grandfather John Hackney left to right: Patricia Slone Belcher, John Hackney, Anna Lee Potter. Second row: Gale D. Coleman Owens, Jewell K. Slone Elswick, Johnny Mack Potter, Danny B. Slone and small child Joneda Scott, Little Beaver. 1958

Right: Front row left to right: Harrison Thacker, unidentified, Richard "Cobb" Thacker, Lona Thacker, lady holding baby is Pricey Thacker, baby unknown, last boy on right is Paris Thacker, Sutton, Kentucky. 1900s.

Left: Burgess Slone with mother Martilla Hunt Slone, Mouthcard, Kentucky. Circa 1913

Below: Four generations of Spurlock and Sadie Belcher Family, owners of Belcher General Store and logging company, Belcher Bottom, Belcher, Kentucky. Back row: Sol, Emma Tackett, Cora Damron, Howard Tackett, Hut Justice, Delbert and Rebecca Tackett, Glenna and Clyde Compton, Mildred and Kermit Ramey, Benny Earl, Lannie, Bruce, Latisha, Delbert Jr. and Deborah Tackett, July 4, 1962.

Left: Tom Self Family — Harriett, Tom, Grayson and Irene, Elkhorn City, Kentucky. 1910

Right: The Sparrel Bartley Family – Delphie, Sparrel, Mary and Martha, Dry Fork of Marrowbone. 1920

Below: Ward Family – Ardile, Nevada, Hazel, Corby, Lenville, Bessie Will, Jenny, Gracie, Roy, Leodia and Ed.

Above: Front row left to right: Marion Daniel Ramey, Nancy Polly Ramey, Pricy Ramey and McKenley "Kenny" Ramey. Back row: Bessie Ramey and Cary Smith Ramey. Picture taken around 1914 or 1915.

Right: Butler and Ida Bishop and children Billy, Loretta, Elster and Phyllis.

Left: Kate Williamson and Bart Rowe on their wedding day. Bart was a policeman in Elkhorn City and was later killed in the line of duty. Kate later married Mr. Cross and lived here in Elkhorn City for many years.

Below: Left to right: Senter Family – Standing: Lilly, Augusta and Richmond. Seated: Fleik, Myrtle, Madison Lee, Winnie and Bryan, before 1904

Above: Cedar Grove Regular Baptist Church Little Beaver, Joe Potter, Mary Potter, Mary O'Quinn, Allie Potter holding Isaac, Jr. Martha Potter holding Rushie and Lille Potter. 1918

Left: Clarence, Emily, Geraldine and Dorothy Burke. Note: Old Water Tank in Elkhorn City, in background.

Right: Back row left to right: Clifford, Buna and Otto Coleman. Front row: Grand and Emily Ratliff Coleman and baby Madelyn Coleman Sykes, Dry Fork Marrowbone. 1921

Below: Lawrence Childers Family, Hellier, Kentucky.

Right: 1. Grover Cleveland Ramey, 2. Cora E. Slone Ramey, 3. Roy Columbus Ramey, 4. Ralph Morgan Ramey, 5. Stella Gladys Martin, 6. Rex Ramey, 7. Opal Hazel R. Cool, 8. William Luther (Bun) Ramey, 9. Beulah Mae R. Belcher, 10. Vada June R. McGuire, 11. Gay Nola R. Robinson, 12. Allen Hassel (Bill) Ramey

Left: Back row left to right: Woodrow Rowe, Ervin Rowe, Olga Rowe. Front row: T.O. Rowe, Elkhorn City, Kentucky, early 1920s.

Below: Right to left: Lexie, Kermit, Ines, Amanda and Lavada Reece. 1944

Left: Wallace Family – Front row left to right: Jettie Wallace Elswick, Dewey Wallace, Crede Wallace Ratliff, Ezra Wallace, Sylvia Mullens Wallace, Goldie Wallace Justus, Rachel Wallace Counts, Tom Wallace. Back row left to right: Rufus Stiltner, Solomon Mullins, John L. Wallace, Jessie Childers, William Slone and Charlie Freeman, about 1910.

Above: Thanksgiving Day, 1911. Back row left to right: May Farmer, Cora T. Farmer Artrip, Armina Cantrell, Celia Artrip Coleman. Front row: Tolbert L. Cantrell, Jethro Artrip, unidentified baby, Ed Cantrell, Hiram Albert Cantrell, John A. Cantrell, unidentified, Ashcamp, Kentucky.

Right: Clevenger's – Grover, Bob, Tina and Grandma Louvada.

John Wesley Childers Family – 7th from left is Flem Childers and 6th from left is wife Maude Moore Childers. Circa 1910

Above: Left to right: Victoria Reed Ramey and Abraham Lincoln Ramey, unidentified Ramey, Louisa E. Ratliff Ramey (sitting in rocker), Dixie Ramey, William Eli Ramey, Evelyn Ramey (sitting far right), Hylton, Kentucky. 1920s

Right: Left to right: Thornsberry Family – Eddie, John and Roma holding Nina, Russell Street, Praise (Elkhorn City). 1944

Above: John Albright, Grace Albright, Jeremy Coleman being held by grandmother Elaine Scott, Marrowbone Creek.

Left: Alice Belcher Salyer holding son Curt, Elkhorn City. 1915

Vinson Belcher Family – Homer, Louisa (mother), Gracie, Bessie, Ray, Elsie, Hyman and Vinson (father). Vince was Justice of the Peace for a number of years, Beaver Creek, Kentucky. Circa 1920

Above: Front row left to right: Verna Brushwood, Charles Brushwood. Back row left to right: George Potter, Ernie Potter, Rushie Potter, George Edward Brushwood, Alice Potter and Isaac Potter. 1921

Left: Left to right: Standing Betty Jane Potter, unidentified. Sitting: Martha Potter. 1920s.

Right: Sidna Potter Daniel, Bertha Potter, Jewell, Lillie Potter Sturgell, Martha Potter Potter, Rushie Potter, Ernie B. Potter, George W. Potter, Joseph Potter and Isaac Potter, Dayton, Tennessee. Circa 1939

Left: George and Elizabeth Ramey Family – 2. Vada Ramey, 3. Italy Ramey, 4. Lasil Ramey, 5. Maudie Ramey, 6. Bud Ramey, 7. Henry Wilson Ralmey, 8. Melvina (Millie, Henry's wife), 9. Turner (baby in lap), 10. George Ramey, Jr., 11. George Ramey, Sr., two little boys between Grandpa and Grandpa and Grandma 12. Jennings Ramey (in back) and 13. Johnny Ramey (in front), 14. Elizabeth Looney Ramey, 15. Virgie (in her lap is Bud's daughter), 16. Lula Ramey. Missing in picture are: Frances Ramey, Florence Ramey, Joseph Nelson (died young)

Right: Left to right: Randy Chaney, Cindy Anderson Chaney and Cecil Chaney.

66

Left: Elkhorn City Railroad Station Elmployees C&O/ CCO – Front row left to right: Frank Loar, Lige Mullins, Cecil Owens, George Smith, Ben Ward, Paris Mullins, Taw Owens (father of Cecil Owens). Back row left to right: Claude Miller, J.E. Rozer, Joe Meade and Lon Roberts. 1921

Clinchfield Railroad Employees – Last day of operation of Elkhorn Yard. Front row left to right: Roy Owens, C.A. Vanover, Lonnie Johnson, Robert Sanders, Morris Wallace, John Adkins, Bill Powell, Clarney Mullins, Alf Edwards, Ira Haynes. Back row left to right: Randall Belcher, Johnny Moore, Chick Spradlin, A.N. Stafford, Harold Slone. Employees missing in photo: Joe Barrowman, Leonard Mullins, Bob Matney, Ervin Matney, Hubert Spradlin, Dale Ratliff, J.B. Ratliff. April 1981

U.M.W.A. Miner's Reunion – Bottom row left to right: Elmer Coleman, Lee Robinson, Reed Damron, Jimmy Dale Sanders. Top row: "Pete" Stalker, "Popeye" Robinson, Trimble Coleman, Edison Wright and grandson Kenny O'Quinn, Darvin Clevenger, Joe Coleman, Julius Prater and Worie Thacker. Taken at Fish Ponds Park, June 13, 1984

HILLBILLY SQUARE DANCERS – 1st row left to right: Willa and Kelver Stiltner, 2nd row: Janice Clevinger, Arlene Stiltner, Glema Stiltner, Tava Sue Stapleton, Elnore Little, Debbie Coleman, 3rd row: Russell D. May, Bill Joe Stiltner, Jim Stapleton, Carmel Stiltner, Butch Clevinger and Donnie Coleman.   1979

Industry

Left: Grenough Coal Company, Leander Castle with jacket. 1911

Below: Yellow Poplar Lumber Company Log Loader used by the lumber company. Many of the local men worked for this Lumber Company, Bartlick, Virginia. 1909

Allegheny Coke Ovens, early 1920s

Left: Coal Car Derailment at Hellier, Kentucky. 1930s

Left: Feds Creek Ferry Boat built by Ance Rowe. 1933

Below: Jeff May and Roland Lee coming home from the coal mines. Pond Creek Street, Draffin, Kentucky. Circa 1940

Above: Ronald Adkins, Mike Adkins L & M Trucking Company, Inc. in June 1976. Hauled coal from Johnson Bros. to Hawkins tipple in East End of Elkhorn City in early 1970s thru mid 1990s. (Submitted by Vickey Adkins, Regina, Kentucky)

Right: Dr. Goebel Newsom showing off a pair of hunting dogs and Log Sweeney showing off a racoon that was a good source of food for the mountain people.

Left: Ray Rose, Russell Fork Coal Company, Little Beaver Creek. Ray was later killed on the job.

Below: Edgewater Coal Company, early 1920

Above: Early construction of Fishtrap Dam, 1965-1966

Left: East Elkhorn City Railroad Yard. First row left to right: Patsy Mullins, Nolen Mullins, Doc Maynor, Andrew Hall and Worley Potter. Second row left to right: Fontie Maynor, Cameron Taylor, John Ratliff and John Taylor, Elkhorn City, Kentucky. Circa 1910

Right: View of Wolfpit, Kentucky. The McKinney Steel Inc. Coal Mining Camp in the early 1900s.

Coke ovens operation, Allegany, Kentucky.

Coal tipple – Hellier area

Right: Construction of Carson Coal Tipple on Ohio Street.

Left: Marrowbone Depot and Coal Dock, Pike County, Kentucky. 1947

Alleghany Coke Ovens on left of picture. Early 1920s

Coal Fired Power Plant at Allegany, Kentucky. 1920s

Left: Front row left to right: Alec Prater, unidentified, Rufus Robinson, Verlon Damron, unidentified and Bill Kenny. Second row: Alf Adkins, unidentified, Ballard Justice, Everett Keene, Willard Kenny, Voll Adkins and Ray Gillespie. Third row: Aril Prater, John Justice, Harry Ratliff, unidentified and John Prater. Fourth row: Clarence Arnold, Mine Owner, Author Scott, Willie Prater, Leonard Robinson, Perry Prater, Hobert Hopkins, Tom Keene, unidentified. Taken on Dry Fork of Greasy Creek, Kentucky. Circa 1940

Left: William May, Pond Creek, Draffin. Coming home from the coal mines. 1950s

Below: Business Area Hellier, Kentucky, 1930s

Above: The Grenough Coal Company before 1920, Hellier, Kentucky.

Right: Cecil Coleman taken in 1936. Old Federal Mines, Elkhorn City, Kentucky.

Right: Arch Graves and Jenny Preston Graves standing at entrance to Edgewater Mines.

Below: Alleghany Coke Ovens, 1920s

Above: Mining camp at Hellier, Kentucky, 1929

Left: An unidentified Coal Miner in the early 1900s just wanted to show the type of Dinner Bucket, Carbide Light, Cap, Shoes and Clothes that was worn by the typical coal miner.

Left: Madison Lee Senter Drug Store on Pine Street, Elkhorn City, Kentucky. 1920s

Right: Edgewater Coal Company Payroll Office

Compliments of Mountain Enterprises, Inc.

COMPLIMENTS OF

ELSWICK CONSTRUCTION COMPANY, INC.

AND

B & R CONSTRUCTION COMPANY, INC.

Owned and operated by people PROUD of their EASTERN KENTUCKY HERITAGE

Compliments of Tim Belcher, Attorney

People

Left: Left to right: Dr. G.W. Newsom, Bill (Wig) Ratliff, Joel Coleman and Noah Owens.

Below: Carl Mullins, Coal Miner, Elkhorn City, early 1940.

Dorothy Burk, Bridge Street. Tom Self's Hardware in background.

Right: Kentucky Casebolt Damron Compton and Mary Compton Stephens... Note the old wash tub on table possibly for washing clothes or canning jars.

Above: Graddy Potter

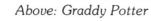

Right: Early Clevinger and Lennie Mercer

Left: Elaine Scott, mother of Deborah Coleman, Levisa Fork, 1944

Above: Clarence Burke and Jus Ratliff on old bridge in Elkhorn City, Kentucky. 1939 or 1940.

Left: Jefferson Davis Slone, Little Beaver Creek, 1940s

Right: Left to right: Ina Mae Rowe, Louise Rowe and Philip Epling in front of Caudill Ward building. They were all bookkeepers for Caudill Ward Coal Company.

Above: Dewey Ramey, son of Calvin Ramey, son of Asbury Ramey, son of Mosey Ramey, son of William Ramey.

Right: Bev Wallace (left) and Landon Potter (right). Two necessities for mountain men, their pistol and their banjo. Bluehead, Kentucky, 1898

Left: Ed Rowe and Gene Rowe sons of Lon and Flossie Rowe

Above: Rose Rowe Wright about 1900s, Russell Street, Elkhorn City, Kentucky.

Left: Mrs. George W. Mullins (left) and Mrs. Autre D. Jackson (right) taken around 1942.

Right: Left to right: Unidentified Potter with her daughter, Cora Clevinger Ramey, Charles Lathram. Back of River View in Elkhorn City.

Above: Florence and Audrey Potter, Elkhorn Creek, early 1950s.

Lawrence Childers on left.

Left: George Stewart and Earl Cure, 1919

Above: Cougar Den 1930-1940, left to right: Dave Ramey, Bill (Wig) Ratliff Owner and Charles W. Ratliff — Russell Street, Elkhorn City.

Bonnie Ride and Berneice Potter, Elkhorn Creek

Right: Tommy Sykes, Bill Hamilton and Don Slone Breaks Park about 1956

Above: Mart Ratliff owner, old ferry in Elkhorn City, Kentucky.

Right: Orlena Deskins 1950s. Front of restaurant in Elkhorn City

Left: David D. Jackson, Elkhorn Street, 1940

Above: Spurlock Belcher, first postmaster at Belcher, Kentucky. He was also a merchant. Son of G.W. and Mary A. Polly Belcher. This picture courtesy of his granddaughter Goldenia Ward Frazier.

Left: Helen Lee (left) and her aunt Christine Lee (right), Pond Creek, Draffin. 1960s

Right: Gay Senters standing on the swinging bridge at Pond Creek, Draffin, Kentucky.

Above: E.B. Bingham, Enos Bart Bingham campaign poster for election to Kentucky State Representative.

Right: Cora Clevinger and Hester Clevinger Potter

Left: Cline Jackson, Elkhorn Street, Elkhorn City, 1938 or 1940

Above: L.E. Rowe, 1940s Republican candidate for Justice of Peace

Left: Katie Ramey Thacker taken on CCC Road Sycamore, Kentucky. 1930s

Right: Nancy Victoria Dunn at John Moore's Branch, 1930s

Below: Left to right: Dave Powell, Rosa Emalene "Dude" Powell, Cary Smith Ramey, Ida-Bell Watson Ramey and Malila Watson. Picture take in 1928 or 1929.

Right: Back of River View Mansion built on 7ᵗʰ Street, Elkhorn City, KY. Early mansion which later burned. Otto Polley.

Left: William Earl Thacker CCC Road at Sycamore, Kentucky. 1930

Below: Lula Farmer, Bridge Street, Elkhorn City, Kentucky

Left to right: Ben Wright, Daniel Wright, Frank Wright, Booker Wright, Benton Wright and Charley Wright.

Right: Cora Polley Ramey (left) and Lucille Parsons (right) in front of Mrs. Ramey's house on Main Street. 1950s

Above: Gerold (Bob) Clevinger son of J.W. Clevinger

Right: Woodrow Potter

Left: Left to right: Eula Hylton, Rushie Mullins unidentified, Hazel Mullins and Faye Belcher Hylton home on Little Beaver Creek near Elkhorn City, 1935

Above: Grandpa Milton Ward, 1925, son of William Ward and Nancy Thompson.

Left: Florida Hackney and Oscar Jackson, Elkhorn City, Kentucky. 1942

Right: Jollene Childers and Gloria Childers playing guitar, Ruth Childers standing in back.

Below: Left to right: Mae Potter, Gus Potter, Roma Hackney and child Allen Wright, Potter Flats. 1930s

Autie "Pop" Jackson and Ellis Jackson, Jackson General Merchandise. First store built in Elkhorn City. It was on Main Street.

Left: Left to right: Carmen Ramey and Rex Ramey, Right Fork of Little Beaver Creek near Elkhorn City. Cousins and great fisherman. Early 1950s

Below: Left to right: Dave Ramey, Bill (Wig) Ratliff, Penny Mullins, ____ Loar and Dave Ratliff, Main Street, Elkhorn City, Kentucky. Showing off their catch.

Dr. John Tilden Deskins (1881- 1957). Dr. Deskins was our local Dr. For many years and left many fond memories when he passed. His wife was also one of faithful women who helped to establish a congregation of the Elkhorn City Church of Christ (Christian) in Elkhorn City. Elkhorn City, Kentucky. 1930.

Right: Noah Shannon Owens and James H. Stewart, Brothers in the Old Regular Baptist Church... NOTICE THE HOB NAILED SHOES.

Above: Mallie Bartley Clevinger

Right: Nellie Ramey Tackett, Dunleary, Kentucky. Nellie served many years as clerk of Elkhorn City and her husband Jack also served the city much of his life. Nellie did the work of two people at the city office and all without the benefit of computers. (Photo courtesy of their daughter, Jeffery Tackett)

Left: Pricey Childers Davis, vegetable garden in background. A necessity for food.

Above: Alice Potter Powell, Elkhorn City, Kentucky. 1930s

Left: Fred Wallace, died 1935, father of Elster Wallace

Martha Potter Vanover

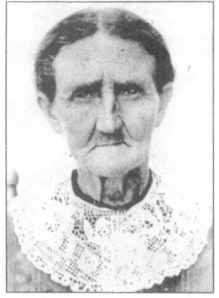

Crit Smallwood

Eliza Moore Bentley Ramey (1855-1927). Daughter of Mary Polly Clevenger and Isaac "Littley Ike" Junior Moore. She married James Bentley and they had 5 children. James was killed at age 38 in a logging accident. She married William Ramey Son of Moses and Jane Fuller Ramey about 1888. They had 2 children, Adam Q. Ramey and a baby just called Infant Ramey who died one day after birth.

Jim Ward, grandson of Milton Ward, died 1943

Jeff Tackett, Elkhorn City

Flora Hackney Slone taken at Elkhorn City Cemetery.

Elkhorn City Area Heritage Council, Inc. Members

Left: Officers of the Elkhorn City Area Heritage Council, Inc. Left to right, back: Terry Thompson, Treasurer; standing in front of Terry is Debbie Coleman, Secretary; Nina Aragon, Vice-President; Timothy D. Belcher, President.

Right: Board Members left to right: Renee Kendrick, Rodney Potter, Nick Marinaro, Neil Potter, Wendall Ward; two missing, Peggy Sykes and Jim Stapleton.

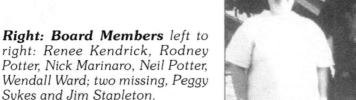

Left: Elkhorn City Area Heritage Council, Inc. Members front row, left to right: Jimmy Lee, Emalene Lee, Renee Kendrick, Sarah Coleman, Debbie Coleman; second row: Nina Aragon, Nila Young, Terri Thompson, Jeff Ramey, Mary Anderson, sitting is Elmer Mullins; third row: Jeffery Alson Tackett, Alma Potter, Vickey Adkins; fourth row: Wendall Ward, Brenda Ward, Bill Ramey, Terry Thompson, Timothy D. Belcher; Nick Marinaro, Rodney Potter, Doug Swiney, Neil Potter.

Members not in picture: *Lee Allen, Dean Belcher, Patricia Belcher, Letha Berry, Sarah Blackburn, Fern Carty, Pat Cole, Jeannette Elswick, Hazel Epling, Goldenia Frazier, William Gibson, Larry Hawkins, Elmer Kendrick II, James Rodney Keene, Elmer Keesee, Patricia Keesee, Angelo Marinaro, Frank Marinaro, Joe Marinaro, Linda Masters, Jack Matney, Lonetta Merritt, Juanita Mullins, Billy Powell, Frank Ratliff, Steve Ratliff, Vickie Reid, Ernest Rowe, Jr., Steve Ruth, Mary Sloan, Dannie Slone, Ken Smith II, Wes Spearman, James R. Stapleton, Ron Stiff, Zetta Stumbo, Peggy Sykes, Scott Sykes, Tommy Sykes, Kenton Wallace, Jr. Billy Williams and Glen Young.*

ACT

Artists Collaborative Theatre, Inc.

... As Rich as Life

OUR MISSION
To create, promote, present, and advance cultural exposure to and training in the performing arts for area residents and visitors and to provide educational experiences of our mountain Appalachian heritage through a collaborative effort.

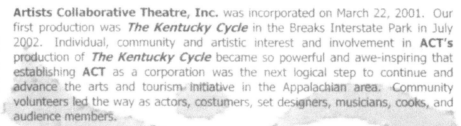

Artists Collaborative Theatre, Inc. was incorporated on March 22, 2001. Our first production was *The Kentucky Cycle* in the Breaks Interstate Park in July 2002. Individual, community and artistic interest and involvement in **ACT's** production of *The Kentucky Cycle* became so powerful and awe-inspiring that establishing **ACT** as a corporation was the next logical step to continue and advance the arts and tourism initiative in the Appalachian area. Community volunteers led the way as actors, costumers, set designers, musicians, cooks, and audience members.

The purpose of **ACT** is to provide the Greater Appalachian area with cultural experiences for both artists and audience attendees through the genre of theatre drama. It provides the public an access to the arts with the opportunity to enhance their appreciation of the arts and, hopefully, will result in a positive outgrowth of enhancement, local pride, self-esteem, confidence, and compassion. It promotes tourism and enhances community development through providing accessible, high-quality, cost effective programs and services and encourages life enrichment opportunities, which can contribute to the advantages for Appalachian people in an increasingly competitive world.

The goals of **ACT**, are to offer and encourage cultural growth, understanding, and exposure to people of differing ethnic, socio-economic, educational, and cultural experiences through the arts. Through the inclusion of and working more closely with area and local educational communities, the under-served populations of Eastern Kentucky and Southwestern Virginia have the opportunity for community participation and positive learning experiences seldom available to the residents of our area

Educational theatre is a foundation of **ACT**. Theatre is one of the strongest vehicles in which young people can develop self-confidence, discover themselves safely and build strong character in order to become readily prepared to better serve a community, a nation, a world. **ACT** is committed to strengthen this option to the youth of Appalachia and to witness the differences in their lives.

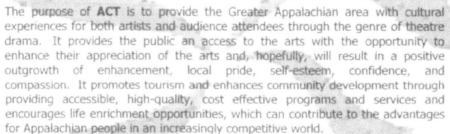

Left: Police Judge, Madison Lee Senter, called "Judge" Senter. Elkhorn City, 1920s

Above: Rake Henry Matney, Deputy Sheriff in 1950s. Late 1940s and 1950s.

Left: Otto and Madelyn Sykes, Elkhorn City Jail, located on Bridge Street, under construction in background. 1940

Left to right: Juss Ratliff, George McCown and John Moore.

Right: The Wards left to right: Zeldon, Roy, Melvina, Eugene and Grandmaw Ginny.

DAV Members, left to right: Claudie Little, Ross Damron, Glenis Mullins, Marvin Clevenger, Goffery Salyers, Elmer Keesee and Lige Counts, Raymond Ramey, Henry Hackney, Elster Robinson, George Justice and Harold Sawyers.

Bobby Lee Merritt, U.S. Army, Viet Nam War

Mack W. Potter 1ˢᵗ on left, WWII

Paul Rogers, U.S. Army, Viet Nam War

David Ratliff, Jr., U.S. Army, Viet Nam War

SMS Elster Robinson, U.S. Air Force, Korean War
and Viet Nam War

Glennis Mullins, WWII, Africa 1943

Ruben Potter and Mart Wallace, WWI

Edward Rowe, Jr. served 14 years in service died in
1984 at age 41

Virgil "Teddy" Hackney, U.S. Army, Viet Nam War

Willie B. May, WWII

William Edward "Eddie" Thornsberry, U.S. Army, Viet Nam War

Clinard Kendrick, Navy, WWII

James Carl Adkins, WWII

Elster Wallace, Japan Occupation Forces end of WWII

Landon Clevinger, WWI

Otis Hackney, WWII

Michael Aragon, U.S. Army during Gulf War

Jessie Stacy, WWII

Edgar Elswick, ROTC

John Edward Aragon, U.S. Army, Gulf War

Virgil Kendrick, WWII

Lewis Ratliff and Jeff Ratliff, Fort Knox, Kentucky, WWI, 1918

Walter E. Coleman, WWII, India 1942-43

Guy Potter, WWII

Berl Childers, WWI

Elwood Potter, Jr., U.S. Army 1960-63

William T. Epling and Elcie Epling, WWII

Dr. Elijah "Lige" Potter, WWI

Pvt. Mart Wallace Obitruary, WWI

Lawrence Childers, WWI

Roland Ramey and Woodrow Ramey, WWII

Charles Hawkins, U.S. Army, WWII

Neil Potter, U.S. Air Force 1962-1966

Rex Ramey, WWII

Ernie Potter, WWII

Julius Ramey, WWII

Front row left to right: Denver Bailey and Richard Deel, WWI, 103 Years, Haysi, Virginia. Standing in back is Buster Varney.

Olida Hawkins, WWII

Thomas Thacker, born 1824, Civil War Prisoner, Rock Island, Illinois 1862-1864

Willie Belcher, son of H.G. and Victoria Hackney Belcher, WWI

Melvin Potter, WWII

Roy Ward, WWI

Modes of Transportation

Left: Cataldo Marinaro, Elkhorn City, Kentucky. 1915

Below: Left to right: Lucille Senters, Sue Davis, Peggy Davis at W.B. Mays Store at Draffin, Kentucky. 1960s

Passenger trains were a way of transportation. Trains were also used to deliver mail.

Left to right: Henry Ramey and unidentified man, Little Beaver Creek, Elkhorn City, Kentucky. 1900

Rushie Hawkins standing by her Model T Ford. Elkhorn City, Kentucky. 1930

Harry Colen

Jim and Beatrice Biliter, 1936

Right: Alvin Bartley,
Edgewater, Kentucky

Left: Left to right: Coleen Hall, Jackie Senters, Johnny
Senters, Sue Stewart, Road Creek, Kentucky. 1962

Schools, Bands & Athletes

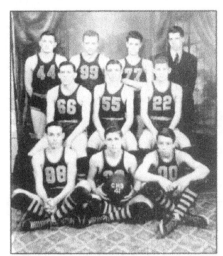

Cumberland High School Basketball Team 1940-41. Left to right: Pete Ramsey No.88, Tugave Coleman with ball in his hands, Zeb Blankenship No. 00, Roshal Amburgey No. 66, Eugene Potter No. 55, ___ Wallace No. 22, Elmer Hall No.44, Earl Hill No.99, Nick Marinaro No. 77, Tilden Deskins with suit on.

Below: Elkhorn City High School Band, 1964-65

Elkhorn City High School and Gym

Right: Beaver Creek Grades 1-7, Eva Belcher teacher, 1947-48.

Elkhorn City Jr. High School County Champions 1978 or 1979. Back row left to right: Tim Belcher, James Hawkins teacher, Marvin Miller. Front row left to right Edward Crum, Craig Kendrick and Eric Ratliff. Not pictured Tim Owens coach helper.

Upper Pond School, Draffin 1950s, Evelyn May (front of line)

Hilton Grade School, 1928

Left: Elkhorn City Grade School, Chester Damron's seventh grade class, 1954-55.

School/Dwelling Grassy Creek, Kentucky

The Lower Pond School House at Draffin, Kentucky. A two room School House.

Hellier High School Students, 1930s

Left: Teacher Mr. Castle, front row left to right: A. Junior Ratliff, Elster Morton, Ola Ray Coleman, Joe Howell, Ravene Farmer. Back row left to right: Delbert Anderson, Lester Ratliff, Franklin Hatfield, Seldon Thacker and Clayton Spears.

Right: Little Beaver Creek School about 1952

ELKHORN CITY COUGARS. Left to right: James Wright, Alec Adkins, Bill Harvey Johnson, unidentified, Morris Wallace, Jimmy "Frog" Cantrell, Billy Ray Conley, Laythe Sykes, Waco Day, Goebel Rush Thacker and Elmer Belcher, Jr.

1941-42 Cumberland High School Basketball Team. First row left to right: Frank Marinaro, Bug Wallace, Bill Ramey, Richard Jackson, Walter Ramey, Eugene Coleman and Zeb Blankenship. Back row: Goebel Newsom, Jr., Pete Ramsey, Eugene Potter, Bob Wright, Elmer Hall, E.H. Nichols and Dick Looney, Coach.

Right: First Football Team, Cumberland High School, Elkhorn City, Kentucky. 1948

Left: Hellier School Children, August 28, 1916

Cumberland High School Play, H.M.S. Pinafore. 1939

Below: Cumberland High School Basketball Team, 1940. 00 - Bill "Gollie" Ramey, 11 - Homer "Chokie" Ratliff, 22 - Pete Ramsey, 33 - Edward Crum, 44 - Eugene Potter, 77 - Ervin "Eagle" Coleman, Manager back left Harry Blake Meade, 88 - Elmer "Humpy" Hall, 99 - Ros "Soup" Amburgey, Coach - Herman "Si" Ramey.

Above: Cumberland High School Facultly. First row: Ocie Ramey, Della Stapleton, Hazel Belcher and Donald Elswick. Second row: Bessie Ramey, Grady Martin, Avery Lewis and Professor McVeight. Third row: Norma Ross and Charlene Coleman. 1930s

Right: First 8th grade graduating class of Cumberland - Class 1938. First row left to right: Nelson Castle Jr., Imogene Hackney, Frank Marinaro, Fanny Belle Ingram, Ted Barrowman, Hazel Wright, Eugene Coleman, Ray Gordon Roberts, Juanita Haynes, Walter Ramey, Richard Jackson and Ruby Nell Ratliff. Second row: Grace Belcher, Virgie Ann Runyon, Joanna Polley, Anna Rae Belcher, Alma Wallace, Etta Marie Smith, Bill Ramey, Anna Rae Wallace, Rusby Belcher, Hester Polley, Nell Marie Ramey, J.O. Johnson and Ray Bailiff. Third row: Goebel Newsom, Pete Ramsey, Eugene Potter, Velma Childers, Sara Smith, Fredreck Stapleton, Edward "Chick" Spradlin and William Rowe.

Left: Grapevine Grade School, Florene Adkins Ramey center and Annie Justice in front. 1915

Old Hellier High School. Hellier Grade School was built in 1918, by the Edgewater Coal Company at the cost of $30,000.00 and furnished it to the Hellier District for use. In 1921, some High School work was offered. In 1926 a three year high school was approved. In September 1927 became the first four year accredited high school out of the county seat of Pikeville.

Above: Girls Basketball Team, 1936. Elkhorn City High School. Eva Rowe Powell and Nell Tackett Elswick are among the group.

Left: Cumberland High School Senior Class. Katherine Mullins, teacher. First row left to right: Mary Jo Ratliff, Betty Salyer, Leah Dane Runyon, Gerald Ratliff, Nina Sanders and Katherine Mullins. Second row: Charlie Ratliff, Curtis Puckett, Billie Jo Whitaker, Nell Tuffs, Loraine Salyers, Parthernia Rowe and Katherine Wright. Third row: Zetta Ratliff _____, Burns Wright, Thomas Slone, Virginia Strickland. Back row: Erman Stapleton, Jim Bob Sanders, Waburn Starnes, Bobby Mason Ramey, Fred Slone and Paul Stiltner.

Right: Arthur Mullins' homeroom class, Elkhorn City, Kentucky. 1960

Left: First School in Elkhorn City, 1908

Right: Cumberland High School Faculty, early 1950s. First row: Principal James V. Powell, Katherine Mullins, Madge Mullins, Catherine Sanders, Opal Belcher, Alpha Thacker and Inez Elswick. Second row: Chester Damron, Joyce Sanders, Ruth Sanders, Maxie Stiltner, Roxie McCown and Della Stapleton. Third row: unidentified, unidentified, Nina True, Clyde Hunter, Eva K. Powell, Jeanetta Ford, Hester Clevinger. Top row: Arthur Mullins, Earl Slone, Willa Ann Looney, Clyde Mullins, Mr. Tackett and Gertrude Rowe.

Left: Little Beaver Grade School, teachers Clinard Ramey and Mason Ramey. 1930s

Right: Potter Flat's School, 1917

Left: Beaver Creek Grades 1-3. Top row left to right: Eva Belcher Stapleton, unidentified, Joy Belcher, Claude Clevinger, Patty Potter, Randal Slone, Sue Ramey and Gene Belcher. Second row: Bennett Adkins, Betty Swiney, Dempsey Belcher, Rebel Belcher, Elwood Potter, Jr. and Nadine Cool. Third row: Zetta Hogston, Neil Potter, Sue Potter, Doug Belcher, Loretta Hawkins, Wesley Ramey, Cassie Potter and Blake Adkins. Fourth row James O. Potter, Nadine Clevinger, Russell Adkins and Herman Ramey, 1948-1949.

Right: Millard Grade School, 8th Grade, 1954.

Dunleary School, north of Elkhorn City. Group includes Georgia Stacy and Clara Holley. About 1921

Methodist Church Sunday School. Front: Carmen Ratliff 11, Peggy Johnson, ___ Burk, unidentified child in front, next four girls unidentified. Back: Maretta Fraley, 2 unidentified women. Teachers: Virginia Elswick Rogers, Lois Ann Ratliff, Landen Elswick Jr., last Bonnie Mae Wallace.

Right: Elkhorn City High School, Sophomores, 1954-55.

Left: Elkhorn City Cheerleaders, 1956. Mary Ellen Potter, Loretta Ratliff, Barbara Bartley, Anna Sue Webb and Sue Mullins.

Cumberland High School Graduating Class, 1940s

Left: Elkhorn City Grade School, Acy Childers 8th Grade Class, 1955-56.

Left: Cumberland High School Graduating Class, 1930

Below: Cumberland High School Seniors, 1932

Above: Hellier High School Basketball Team Coach Arthur "Mock" Mullins at far right. About 1940.

Right: Elkhorn City High School, Freshman, 1954-55.

W.P.A. Projects

W.P.A. Sewing Class at J.D. Wright Store. Group includes Haddie Castle, Alice Stacy, Burnie Potter, Bessie Stanley, Minnie Rowe, Leenia Looney, Alice Hylton, Georgia Stapleton, Maggie Rowe, Arizona Short and Luamma Rowe. About 1940

Below: WPA Project Fish and Games Club House still under construction in 1936. On right is Frank Loar, Brick layer.

Another W.P.A. Project, The Fish Hatchery located at Elkhorn City (Praise, Kentucky) in the 1930s, stocked the streams of Pike County with over forty thousand bass annually, under the direction of the Pike County Fish and Game Protective Association.

Below: W.P.A. Crew working on stone bleachers at Elkhorn City Ball Park and Elkhorn City Cemetery. Frank Loar front right

Group of N.Y.A. girls from Elkhorn City, Virgie and Pikeville, Kentucky. Bessie Ramey director 1943. Group includes Ruthie Potter, Ivel Hackney, Essie Stapleton, Thelma Robinson, Bessie Ramey, Alpha Rose, Ampal Rose and _____ Wright.

Right: CCC Camp on Elkhorn Creek. 1941-1942

Memorials & Tributes

Erin Scott Anderson
February 9, 1990 - June 14, 2003

School and Organizations

He participated in the Academic Team for five years. Erin won the Junior High School Spelling Bee. He had always been and accomplished speller and an expert in phonics of new words. He was in Gifted and Talented classes for two years but when he went to the Pikeville High School he chose to forgo GT for Band. Erin played a coronet for two years. He was currently in the Junior High Band where he was also in the Pep Band. Erin was a member of the Boy Scouts of America. He started when he was in the first grade as a Tiger Cub and was a Boy Scout second-class working toward his Eagle Scout. Erin held a life membership in the Little People of America, an honorary member of the Elkhorn City Heritage Council and a member of Experimental Aircraft Association (EAA).

...these are a few of his favorite things...

Lover of Airplanes: Erin loved anything about airplanes. Erin flew his first plane at two years of age. On the way to Maryland in a small private airplane (I don't remember the make but Erin would) he got his first taste of taking the reins. He was hooked from then on. He was an avid follower of the Wings Channel. He had participated for three years in the Aviation Camp held in Lexington, Kentucky at the Bluegrass Airport. He and his father's plans for the summer of 2003 were to take ground school at Hatcher Field Airport. This was the first step to a Pilots License, a goal that Erin was anxious to achieve.

Favorite Foods: For dinner he preferred steak served with generous supply of Al sauce, baked potato loaded in butter and lots of sour cream, salad with only lettuce (no tomatoes, cucumbers or peppers) served with Red Wine Vinaigrette salad dressing or Ranch dressing. Second and third favorites would be spaghetti and shrimp scampi. (Oysters on the half shell were a close runner-up). For breakfast well… None! (Erin preferred to dine after he had been awake for several hours. Unless he happened to be at the Rusty Fork Cafe in which case he would make an exception and eat early.)

Favorite Vacation: Anywhere with his Dad was Erin's favorite vacation. Most preferred was a good air show, either Oshkosh Air Show in Oshkosh, Wisconsin or Fun-in-the-Sun in Ocala, Florida. A close second would be the Little People of America conventions. This is a place where he could roam a large hotel with his close friends and 'buds.' They would just hang, go swimming or attend the banquets and dances held. The convention allows a feeling of independence that he would not be able to experience at any other time.

Reflections: Erin was blessed to have had wonderful friends; people who continue to remember him and miss him. Erin was 13 years old when he passed away. He was having surgery on his spine. This was his twenty-third surgery, his second spinal surgery when complications arose during surgery.

The things we will remember most… flying, speeding on your walker, spelling, and the twinkle in your eye. We will miss you in all things, but especially when we see an airplane fly by on a summer day. And sometimes when I look up in the sky and see the jet streams of many airplanes that have flown about. I will imagine you have been out writing in the sky.

His parents have not yet learned how to live. We have discovered that we have no use for our arms. There is nothing to hold, hug, or carry that makes any sense.

The emptiness in our hearts is like that of an abyss. We have neither the words nor the proper ordering of them to convey the emptiness that surrounds us.

Erin, thanks for the memories!

Tribute To The Anderson Family
Main Street, Praise, KY

I was born April 23, 1919, in Praise, were Carrie (Jackson) and Seaton Biggs. except for two years our family lived in at Pikeville College Academy. My father Williamson Hardware. He was from (from Elkhorn City) at Pikeville College. garet Record. I was born in the upstairs Elkhorn Street. My parents were living the other side of river what now is known born there in 1923. We attended building for a school - also a music room. out next to the creek. In this building one building. My sister and I walked to school the river.

Leslie played basketball on the team He had three sisters, Fern, Lynn and graduated 1935 and I graduated 1937. He Company. His dad, Perry Anderson, was Dunleary closed.

Mary and Leslie Anderson
50th Wedding Anniversary

KY, and now Elkhorn City. My parents I have lived all my life in Elkhorn City Pikeville. I attended school first two years was a traveling salesman for Ben Greenup, Kentucky and met my mother I had one sister three years younger, Mar- room of the Drummer Building on in two rooms while building our home on as Hatcher Street. My sister Margaret was Cumberland High School, the first brick The gymnasium was a wooden building started the primer and graduated in same around the side of the cemetery next to

for the Cougars, while I was a cheerleader. Sadie. We married August 7, 1937. He was a script writer at Dunleary Mining bookkeeper. Shortly after we married

My grandparents, Autie D. Jackson and Missouri Frances (Mullins) Jackson, came from Jane, Virginia (near Breaks) to Praise, Kentucky. He built the first General Merchandise Store on Main Street, two wooden ones burned. The third, a brick building, is the one that United Steel Workers Local Union occupies. Below the Jackson General Merchandise were Caudill Ward, Joe and Bill Powell Restaurant which served good hotdogs, hamburgers or a bar of Milky Way candy. Next was Bill Rowe's Barber Shop; on the corner was the Wholesale Grocery Building that my grandfather Autie Jackson and his son Jim owned. There were two telephones on Main Street one in the wholesale and other in Elswick Hotel. They had to have everything shipped in by railroad. Across the street, which was dirt, was the Elswick Hotel, the Bank Building, G.W. Mullins' home, Tom Self Hardware, Fount Mullins Watch Repair, Dr. Deskins' Office, Ferd Sanders' Barber Shop and a two story building which burned and three people died. Nothing was ever built back on it to this day.

The occupation was coal industry, railroad, school teachers, and logging. The Depot was at end of Main Street. We had C & 0 Railroad coming north from Ashland, Kentucky. The train left in morning and came in afternoon and back at night. The CC&O from the south to Irwin, Tennessee and Spartanburg, South Carolina it would leave in morning and return at night. Some of the men that worked on the railroad moved with families to Elkhorn City while others stayed in boarding houses or one of two hotels, Elswick Hotel and Barrowman Hotel. It was always fun to meet the trains just to see who got off.

Dr. G.W. Newsom and family moved to Praise in 1930, they lived in Roland Elswick house on Elkhorn Street. He bought the bank building for office. Autie Jackson bought a drug store in Grundy, Virginia and hauled the fixtures to Elkhorn City through the Breaks on a dirt wagon road. My mother and daddy rented the building for the "Drug Store" they operated it for two years; daddy died June 9, 1932 at age 34. My mother was left with two girls ages 13 and 10; it became too much for her so Ray and Florence Jackson operated it until Leslie and I bought it in 1938.

My sister Margaret married Jimmy Coleman from Marrowbone, he was a school teacher. They were married February, 1938, and she died in September at age 16.

Dr. Newsom bought the house of G.W. Mullins next door; built a brick building which was the Drug Store and White Star operated by Roy and Shirley Looney and his office on second floor. The Bank Building was then the Post Office where Ralph and Bessie Ramey worked. It was about this time we had to change name Drug Store to Cumberland Confectionery and we did not have a pharmacy, only sold patented medicines. Dr. Newsom built a two-story brick house on Main Street next to General Store across from office. It was about this time 1938 that Autie Jackson built the first theater with sound beside the Wholesale. Jiffy Grill was beside it operated by George Mullins. The theater was first operated by a man from Norton, VA named Murphy, thus the name. Later, Ray and Florence Jackson operated it.

Beginning with 1940 things began to boom, the theater was bought by Emmit Belcher. There were live performances by Minnie Pearl, Tex Ritter, Roy Acuff, Wild Bill Hickoff, Lashloure, and Flat and Scruggs. People came to the Cumberland Confectionery, White Star, Theater and Dr. Newsom. We had fountain Cokes, ice cream patent medicines, cosmetics, and jewelry. We bought the first ice machine. Bus ran from Pikeville, we sold tickets. We had juke box and pinball machine, After every basketball game the people came to "play over the game."

Our first son Leslie Seaton was born March 21, 1941, on a Sunday, December 7, 1941, I had gone to the movie with him. I walked in business and Leslie was listening to the radio. He said "the Japanese has just bombed Pearl Harbor." We were stunned as Wick Ratliff, Bill Powell and Carmen Wallace were there. Many were killed on ships but they were safe. Many boys from our area enlisted; we had pictures of them in uniforms in our store window. Food and gasoline were rationed. Everyone listened to radio for news. Leslie was drafted but didn't pass physical exam due to his heart. Our second son Dennis Gene was born September 19, 1944. The war ended 1945. Business remained good until early fifties. Fran and Greg (twins) were born August 28, 1953. We sold the Cumberland Confectionery in 1955.

Leslie retired from Pike County Coal in 1982. I retired from Cabinet for Human Resources Department Social Insurance July, 1984. All four sons graduated from University of Kentucky. Dennis Gene married Linda Williams, June 1965. They lived in Lexington. Dennis died August 20, 1975. Leslie Seaton married Nancy Vaughn, September 2, 1967, Union, SC. They had two children Rebecca Jane and Travis Lee. Fran married Pamela Kendrick, May 25, 1974, Elkhorn City Christian Church, they had two girls, Carrie Lindsey and Lesley Kendrick.

The land beyond the Christian Church was undeveloped. In 1945, Leslie and Mary and Evert and Edna Senters bought land and built the first two brick houses. A road from the church by cemetery to hall park was built - named Hatcher Street. Presently homes have been built up the mountain to 7th Street. We moved into our home in May 1946.

Carrie married Shane Robertson, June 7, 1996, in Lexington, they have two children, Corey and Shaelyn. Jane married Henry Petty, Union, SC, they have a daughter, Morgan. Lesley married Jeremy Jones, July, 2003. Leslie died March 14, 2002.

Submitted by Mary B. Anderson.

L-R: Travis, Leslie Seaton, Jane and Nancy Anderson

Leslie Seaton, Mary and Leslie Anderson

Hatcher Street, 1954, l-r: Leslie, Gregg, Fran, Mary, Leslie Seaton and Dennis Gene Anderson standing in front.

Dennis Gene and Linda Anderson

Gregory Ray Anderson

Pam, Fran, Lesley and Carrie Anderson

Travis Lee Anderson

Corey and Shaelyn Robertson

Jane, Henry and Morgan Petty

Lesley and Jeremy Jones

Carrie and Shane Robertson

Tribute to Grandparents of Tim Belcher

Burgess Slone and Flora Hackney Slone at Elkhorn City Cemetery 1929 - Grandparents

Hyman Belcher, Grandfather, died at age 27

Lenore Potter Belcher Adkins, Grandmother and James Carl Adkins, Step-Grandfather

John Hackney and Maggie Bingham Hackney, Great-Grandparents

Tim Belcher

Vinson Belcher and Louisa Potter Belcher, Great-Grandparents

Jefferson Davis Slone and Martilla Hunt Slone, Great-Grandparents

William Landen Potter and Jettie Bartley Potter, Great-Grandparents

Remembering Curt and Lyda Caudill

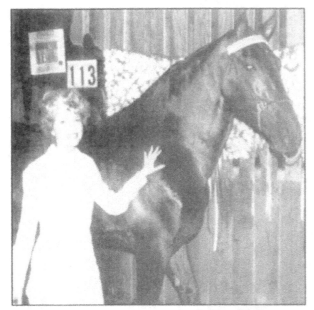

Caudill-Ward Coal Company store and office, Main Street, Elkhorn City, in 1950s: Phillip Epling, Victor Fields, Curt Caudill, Tom Johnson, Ina Mae Rowe. Not Shown: Louise Rowe and Nell Webb.

Above: Lyda Caudill wih her favorite horse Eight Ball. She served on the National Board of Tennessee Walking Horse Exibitors' and Breeders' Association and owned horses that were Kentucky, National and World Champions.

Below: Lyda Caudill was an organizer of Elkhorn City Girl Scouts in the 1940s. She is shown here with a Brownie troop.

Right: Telephone Dial Services came to Elkhorn in 1949. Mayor C.M. Caudill made the first call to the former mayor Dr. A.W. Newsom in Fort Pierce, Florida.

CAUDILL-WARD COAL COMPANY, HELLIER, KY.

The thickness of seams of coal differs largely. Sometimes a very thin seam — less than three feet thick — is mined, but here at the Caudill-Ward mine is a seam of Elkhorn coal that truly makes the producer feel that he "has something." Mr. Curt Caudill stands by the side of a mine car. He has his hat on, and you will notice that the top of his hat is not dirty, for the seam of coal there is thick enough to permit a man to walk upright.

Left: 1945 Photograph of Hellier Mine from Holmes Darst Coal Corp. brochure.

Caudill-Ward had mines at Hellier and at Federal near Elkhorn City.

The Landen and Jettie Elswick Family

Landen Elswick

Jettie W. Elswick

Old house in Elkhorn City, built in 1890.

Landen Elswick Family - Jr., Ray, Joe, Va and Net

Bee W. Wallace

A Tribute To Richard Elswick
(1948 - 2001)

Richard Elswick with son Philip R. Elswick. Richard had a great influence on his son. Philip is presently completing his Doctorate in Chemistry at University of Kentucky.

Richard Elswick and Jewell K. Slone were married on Dec. 31, 1972. Jewell resides in Pikeville, KY with her son Philip.

Richard Elswick graduated from University of Kentucky School of Law in 1972. He was a member of the Kentucky Law Journal, served as captain for three years in the U.S. Army, went into private law practice for four years in Pikeville, was appointed to District Court Bench on January 7, 1980 and held this office until appointed to the Court of Appeal in 1989. He served one year as assistant County Attorney. Richard maintained an office in Pikeville until his death on March 20, 2001.

Throughout Richard's illustrious legal career, he was known as a "lawyer's lawyer and a judge's judge." Widely respected for both his knowledge and his integrity, his counsel was frequently sought by other attorneys. It was a sad day for all those who knew him when he passed away on March 20, 2001. To his wife, Jewell, and his son, Philip, who provided him with unconditional support and encouragement, their immeasurable loss is tempered by the knowledge that Richard was held in the highest regard by his peers.

Richard Elswick
1948-2001

As a father, husband, lawyer and judge, Richard was always prepared because he knew the security of and trusted in the shelter of God. The light of this great man continues to shine, and we who knew him while he was with us in this world are all the better for it.

Left: Richard was appointed as Judge of Kentucky Court of Appeals, March 2, 1989, by Governor Wallace Wilkinson.

Were a star quenched on high,
For ages would its light
Still traveling downward from
the sky.
Shine on our mortal sight.

So when a great man dies.
For years beyond our ken,
The light he leaves behind him
lies
Upon the paths of men

In Loving Memory of the William and Mellie Carraway Hackney Family

L-R: Otis, Florida, William, Roma, Eunice, Mellie, baby standing in front of William is Ivel Hackney.

L-R: Ivel Keisman, Rama Thornsberry, Mellie Hackney (seated), Florida Hall and Eunice McCreary. Mellie Hackney's 99th birthday.

William Hackney was born June 15, 1887, son of Samuel and Melvina Adkins Hackney. Mellie Carraway was born July 19, 1889, daughter of Marion and Surrilda Lee Carraway.

William Hackney and Mellie Carraway were married in Pike County, Kentucky March 13, 1907. They made their home in Buchanan County, Virginia until their third child was born then moved to Elkhorn City, Kentucky. Will Hackney was a Black Smith by trade and a member of the Odd Fellows Organization in Elkhorn City. Mellie Hackney was a house wife, mother and helped organize the Elkhorn City Christian Church. In 1923, Will's appendix ruptured and he died at the age of 36 years old in Richlands, Virginia. He left six (6) children for Mellie to raise. Without any help Mellie Hackney raised six wonderful children. Her two sons served in the military during World War II. Her four daughters worked at different jobs helping their mother supplement the family income. Times were hard, but Mellie managed to raise all her children and live to see many of her great-great-grandchildren born. Mellie Hackney was 99 years and 6 months old at her death. February 6, 1989.

Children of William and Mellie Hackney were:

Florida Hackney, married Curtis Hall and had two daughters, Merneal Hall and Jean Gray Hall.
Otis Hackney, never married
Roma Hackney married John Thornsberry and had two children, a son William Edward "Eddie" Thornsberry and a daughter Nina Jean Thornsberry.
Eunice Hackney married Mack (Otis) McCreary and had four children: Gay N. McCreary, Mack "Buddy" McCreary, Jackie R. McCreary and Patricia A. McCreary.
Ivel Keisman married Jack Keisman and had one daughter, Mary Katherine Keisman.
Virgil Hackney married Syble Belcher and had two sons, Virgil T. Hackney and Eddie Dean Hackney.
William and Mellie Hackney are buried on the Elkhorn City Cemetery with all but one of their six children, Eunice McCreary who is buried in Corbin, Kentucky.

Tribute To Cataldo "Kelly" Marinaro and Maria Costantina Paonessa Marinaro

Written by Kent Marinaro in the 6th Grade

A Young Man's Dream

On January 1, 1886 in Talsano, Italy a baby boy was born. As the years passed the boy couldn't help but to think of what it would be like in America, the country that he had heard so much about.

So in the summer of 1907 at the age of 21, he boarded an ocean liner in Naples, Italy. There were hundreds of people on the ship, all of them wanting a better life in America. The ship was the Vulcania.

After several days at sea, the ship landed at Ellis Island in New York Harbor. The Statue of Liberty was nearby. It took several days to get examinations and papers done so the people could look for work.

From Ellis Island the young man and other Italians went to Buffalo, New York because they heard there was work at Niagara Falls. The young man got a job digging an elevator shaft from the top of the Falls.

The young man and two other immigrants heard that there was more work in West Virginia. After saving their money they went to West Virginia. There were many railroads being built in those days before World War I. The railroad work lasted for two years; it was now 1915.

The young man went to Norton, VA and worked in the coal mines for awhile. Then came an opportunity for him to become a merchant. He had a good business

Back row, l-r: Joe, Mary, Maria, Cataldo "Kelly;" front, l-r: Angelo, Nick and Frank Marinaro

Marinaro Family Reunion 2003

because he was good to people and had the products that most people used. He even baked bread in his ovens and sold it. The young man had done well for himself in Virginia.

In 1919, after World War I, there came to Norton, Virginia, a pretty Italian girl. She was born November 20, 1901 in Gimiliano, Italy. Her name was Maria Constantina Paonessa. In 1920 the young man would take her for his bride. This was a large celebration with many immigrants from Virginia attending the wedding.

The couple moved about 50 miles from Norton, Virginia, to a little town called Elkhorn City, Kentucky. The young Italian couple faced a lot of prejudice because they were the only immigrants in town. The young man bought a block machine and hauled sand from the banks of the Little Sandy River in wagon pulled by a team of horses that he owned. In 1925 the couple moved into their new two-story home.

The building was a busy grocery on the first floor and a loving and happy home on the second floor. Together they raised five children. Angelo, Nick, Frank, Mary and Joseph. All five of the children went to college and became teachers and successful businessmen.

The death of their father came in 1969 at the age of 83. The mother's death came in 1979 at the age of 78. The family now has the five children, 17 grandchildren, 26 great-grandchildren and four great-great-grandchildren.

The baby boy born so long ago in far away Italy was Cataldo Marinaro. He was to be my great-grandfather. As my grandfather told me about him I knew that with a dream, kindness and hard work that anything is possible.

In Memory of Newsom - Wallace Families

Goebel William Newsom Sr.,
Goeble William Newson Jr.,
Virginia Dare Newsom (baby),
Helena Newsom, made in
Kansas, MO, Spring of 1929.

Dr. and Mrs. Goebel Newsom, made at
Elswick Motel – 1948

Snead Wallace Family 1944.
Standing: Remus, Rudale,
Carmel, Eula (Guy's wife),
Kenton, Bug and Anna Rae;
seated: Snead Wallace, RG
"Worm," Bessie Wallace; front:
Morris and Bonnie Mae Wallace

Carmel Wallace and grand-
children, Patrick and Meredith
Wallace, Corbin, KY, 1983

Carmel Wallace

Dr. and Mrs. Goebel Newsome
and
Mr. and Mrs. Cornelius (Snead) Wallace

Dr. Goebel W. Newsome came to Elkhorn City with his wife and their children, Goebel Jr., Helema and Virginia Dare in 1930. After he completed his medical education at Kansas City Medical School in Missouri and his residence at Stevenson Hospital in Ashland, Kentucky, his father paid the first month's rent for an office upstairs in the old bank building on Main Street. He also rented Roland Elswick's house for the family to live in. They had three more children after coming to Elkhorn City. They were Jean Gray, Faye Ann and Randy.

One of his first patients was a young boy 14 years of age, Carmel Wallace, the oldest son of Cornelius (Snead) and Bessie Wallace. There were ten children in their family. Carmel joined the army and was at Pearl Harbor, Guam and other points. When the war was over and he came home, he married Dr. Newsom's daughter, Virginia Dare. They had two sons, Carmel Jr. (Carnie) and Michael Gene. Carnie followed in his grandfather's footsteps and became a doctor also. Carmel and Virginia Dare had two grandchildren, Patrick and Meredith. The Wallace's was one of the early families in Elkhorn City.

Later Dr. Newsom bought the G.W. Mullins home and property beside the bank building. He built a two story brick building. His office was upstairs and the Drug Store and White Star Restaurant was downstairs on the street level. In 1934 he built their home across the street.

He served as Mayor of Elkhorn City for several years. During this time the city purchased their first fire truck, developed the ball part complete with grandstand made out of river rock and lights. He sponsored the city baseball team for several years.

With the help of his personal friends, Gov. Earl Clements and Congressman Carl Perkins, they got the state of Kentucky to build a road to the Breaks, hoping it would open up tourism to the area.

In 1955 during Gov. Happy Chandler's Administration, Goebel Jr., then a member of the Kentucky House of Representatives, was instrumental in working to pass the Legislation Appropriation Bill to fund Kentucky's role in the development of the Breaks Interstate Park. Dr. Newsom was known to be an avid hunter and fisherman. He loved to hike these mountains and he loved this town.

In Memory of George and Mellie Potter Ratliff

George and Mellie Ratliff

Jean Ratliff Prater, Juanita Ratliff and Millie Ratliff

L-R: Rodney Ratliff, George Ratliff Jr., Bobby Ratliff, Foster Ratliff, Jean Ratliff Prater, the late Elmer Ratliff, Thelma Ratliff, Laronne Ratliff, William Ratliff, Imal Ratliff Jackson, Ersel Ratliff, Estes Ratliff, Jack Ratliff, Lester "Coolie" Ratliff.

Dedicated To and In Remembrance of
The Family of Harve and Cora Ratliff

James Harve Ratliff
3/5/1889 – 6/16/1965
*Elkhorn City Cemetery

Cora Lee (Wallace) Ratliff
7/14/1892 – 12/21/1947
*Elkhorn City Cemetery

Harve and Cora were married in the year 1908, had eleven children and 39 grandchildren. Both Harve and Cora are buried in the Elkhorn City Cemetery as are four of their children. Two living children; Charles Ratliff and Evelyn Mays live in Ohio and West Virginia respectively. Five children are buried in other places as shown in the listing.

James Harve Ratliff

Home in Elkhorn City, Elkhorn Street
(Removed in 1990)

Cora Lee Ratliff and granddaughter, Peggy Necamp

Children in Birth Order:

ESTELLE MULLINS
9/29/1910 – 2/18/1950
*Elkhorn City

RUBY CONLEY
7/18/1912 – 7/2/1975
*Elkhorn City

JOHN CLAYTON RATLIFF
7/06/1913 – 2/21/1980
*Ft. Mitchell, KY

PALMER RATLIFF
10/6/1915 – 4/29/1935
*Elkhorn City

WOODROW WILSON RATLIFF
11/7/1917 – 2/24/1979
*Pikeville-Johnson Memorial
Cemetery

EDITH FAY DAMRON
9/5/1919 – 10/1/1974
*Gallipolis, OH

JAMES W. RATLIFF
6/14/1921 – 1/1/1976
*Ft. Mitchell, KY

EARL RATLIFF
4/4/1923 – 7/14/1983
*Elkhorn City

EVELYN M. MAYS
1/6/1925 -

WALTER RATLIFF
6/14/1927 – 3/5/1964
*Gallipolis, OH

CHARLES W. RATLIFF
7/8/1931 -

Daughters listed with Married
Name
*Place of Burial

Index

A

Ackman 30
Adams 22
Adkins 21, 26, 67, 70, 73, 99, 107, 120, 123, 125, 134, 138
Akers 19, 43, 44
Albright 65
Allen 28, 99
Allison 26, 28
Alloway 50
Amburgey 11, 117, 122
Anderson 6, 14, 26, 47, 66, 99, 120, 131, 132, 133
Aragon 99, 108
Arnold 73
Artrip 64

B

Bachman 26
Bailey 113
Bailiff 23, 122
Balding 26
Barke 20
Barrowman 67, 122
Bartley 19, 31, 60, 96, 116, 127, 134
Beavers 23
Belcher 9, 26, 28, 32, 37, 42, 45, 53, 55, 56, 57, 58, 59, 62, 65, 78, 87, 93, 99, 114, 118, 120, 122, 124, 125, 132, 134, 138
Bennette 13
Bentley 40, 56, 98
Benton 15
Berry 99
Bickford 50, 51
Biggs 132
Biliter 116
Billiter 50
Bingham 23, 88, 134
Bird 26
Bishop 60
Blackburn 21, 99
Blair 6
Blankenship 117, 120
Bolton 26
Booth 30
Branham 55
Breeding 36
Bridges 30

Briggs 30, 31
Brown 26
Brushwood 65
Burk 79, 126
Burke 26, 61, 81
Butler 15, 42

C

Cantrell 19, 26, 27, 64, 120
Carraway 138
Carty 99
Casebolt 80
Castle 35, 50, 69, 120, 122, 129
Caudill 18, 135
Chandler 140
Chaney 45, 66
Childers 14, 15, 43, 44, 51, 58, 62, 63, 64, 84, 94, 97, 110, 111, 122, 127
Childres 13
Church 42
Clark 26
Clements 140
Clevenger 64, 68, 98, 103
Clevinger 13, 30, 68, 80, 84, 88, 92, 96, 107, 124, 125
Cole 99
Coleman 23, 26, 31, 34, 39, 56, 62, 64, 65, 68, 74, 79, 81, 99, 109, 117, 120, 122, 132
Colen 116
Colley 57
Compton 26, 59, 80
Conley 120, 142
Cook 44
Cool 62, 125
Counts 63, 103
Cross 26, 61
Crowder 32, 57
Crum 118, 122
Cure 30, 85

D

Damron 26, 41, 59, 68, 73, 80, 103, 119, 124, 142
Daniel 11, 60, 66
Dare 140
Davis 42, 97, 115

Day 120
Deel 113
Denny 28
Deskins 26, 57, 86, 95, 117, 132
Dunn 90

E

Edwards 67
Eicher 23, 24
Elliot 28
Elliott 19
Elswick 5, 26, 28, 29, 30, 46, 49, 52, 58, 63, 99, 108, 122, 123, 124, 126, 132, 136, 137, 140
England 26
Epling 15, 26, 57, 82, 99, 110

F

Farmer 19, 26, 44, 64, 91, 120
Ferris 28
Fields 26, 31, 135
Flanary 26
Ford 26, 30, 124
Fraley 126
Francisco 26
Franklin 38
Frazier 87, 99
Frederick 30
Freeman 44, 63
Fuller 46, 98

G

Gaines 28
Gibson 26, 34, 54, 99
Gillespie 73
Globe 30
Good 26
Grave 75
Gray 41
Gunnells 42

H

Hackney 8, 26, 28, 56, 58, 93, 94, 98, 103, 106, 107, 114, 122, 130, 134, 138
Hall 30, 41, 71, 116, 117, 120, 122, 138

Hamilton 86
Hamm 26
Hatcher 26
Hatfield 47, 120
Hawkins 12, 14, 16, 33, 43, 45, 49, 58, 99, 112, 113, 115, 118, 125
Haynes 67, 122
Herman 55
Hill 117
Hinton 28
Hogston 125
Hollar 30
Holley 8, 32, 126
Holmes 21
Honaker 26, 30
Hopkins 57, 73
Howell 120
Hubbard 50
Hunt 20, 26, 30, 59, 134
Hunter 124
Hutchings 30
Hylton 55, 93, 129

I

Ingram 122

J

Jackson 5, 6, 9, 32, 83, 87, 89, 93, 94, 120, 122, 132
Johnson 17, 23, 47, 67, 120, 122, 126, 135
Jones 133
Justice 59, 73, 103, 123
Justus 63

K

Keathly 30
Keene 73, 99
Keesee 99, 103
Keeton 14
Keisman 138
Kendrick 14, 26, 33, 40, 99, 106, 109, 118, 133
Kenny 73

L

Lathram 84
Lee 5, 18, 26, 41, 46, 70, 87, 99
Lewis 122

Lipps 21
Little 44, 68, 103
Loar 20, 43, 67, 129, 130
Long 30
Looney 6, 9, 29, 46, 66, 120, 124, 129, 132

M

Marinaro 10, 99, 115, 117, 120, 122, 139
Marrs 9
Martin 62, 122
Masters 99
Matney 67, 99, 101
May 46, 68, 70, 74, 106, 118, 142
Maynard 37
Maynor 17, 26, 35, 71
Mays 14, 43, 115, 142
McCown 102, 124
McCreary 138
McFadden 26
McGuire 62
McIntosh 26
McVeight 122
Meade 28, 30, 67, 122
Meadows 56
Menefee 28
Mercer 80
Merritt 99, 104
Miles 12
Miller 67, 118
Moore 40, 64, 67, 98, 102
Morton 120
Mounts 26
Mullens 63
Mullins 9, 14, 16, 26, 34, 38, 39, 40, 52, 63, 67, 71, 79, 83, 93, 95, 99, 103, 105, 123, 124, 127, 128, 132, 140, 142

N

Nave 28
Necamp 142
Neff 26
Newsom 49, 70, 79, 120, 122, 132, 135, 140
Nichols 120

O

Odom 11
O'Quinn 36, 61, 68
Owens 29, 58, 67, 79, 96, 118
Owner 73

P

Palton 30
Paonessa 139
Parsons 92
Peters 29
Petty 133
Pinson 28
Polley 30, 90, 92, 122
Potter 11, 13, 20, 26, 31, 32, 36, 38, 40, 41, 45, 57, 58, 61, 65, 66, 71, 80, 82, 84, 85, 88, 92, 94, 97, 98, 99, 104, 105, 109, 110, 111, 112, 113, 114, 117, 120, 122, 125, 127, 129, 130, 134, 141
Powel 14
Powell 26, 67, 90, 97, 99, 123, 124, 132
Prater 26, 68, 73, 141
Preston 75
Puckett 26, 123

R

Rakes 13
Ramey 6, 8, 11, 17, 18, 19, 21, 26, 30, 31, 32, 35, 39, 53, 55, 56, 59, 60, 62, 64, 66, 82, 84, 85, 89, 90, 92, 95, 96, 98, 99, 103, 112, 113, 115, 120, 122, 123, 125, 130, 132
Ramsey 120, 122
Ratliff 9, 10, 16, 17, 19, 20, 26, 30, 43, 50, 62, 63, 64, 67, 71, 73, 79, 81, 85, 86, 95, 99, 102, 104, 109, 118, 120, 122, 123, 126, 127, 132, 141, 142

Record 132
Reece 12, 36, 63
Reed 64
Reid 99
Ride 85
Roach 26
Roberts 67, 122
Robertson 133
Robinson 15, 26, 62, 68, 73, 103, 105, 130
Rogers 104, 126
Rose 26, 71, 130
Ross 122
Rowe 2, 26, 33, 54, 61, 63, 70, 82, 83, 89, 99, 105, 122, 123, 124, 129, 132, 135
Rozer 67
Runyon 122, 123
Ruth 99

S

Salyer 18, 26, 29, 45, 55, 65, 123
Salyers 57, 103, 123
Sanders 10, 13, 15, 22, 26, 30, 37, 40, 67, 68, 123, 124, 132
Sanstrom 26
Sawyers 103
Scott 55, 58, 65, 73, 81
Seaton 6, 14, 26
Self 23, 26, 59, 79, 132
Senter 26, 36, 40, 56, 61, 76, 101
Senters 88, 115, 116, 133
Short 129
Sifers 44
Simpson 28
Sloan 99
Slone 14, 19, 23, 56, 58, 59, 62, 63, 67, 81, 86, 98, 99, 123, 124, 125, 134, 137
Smallwood 98
Smith 26, 44, 60, 67, 90, 99, 122
Snead 140
Snyder 30
Spearman 99
Spears 34, 47, 48, 120
Spivey 26

Spradlin 26, 40, 67, 122
Stacy 15, 34, 35, 38, 108, 126, 129
Stafford 67
Stalker 68
Stanley 129
Stapleton 17, 68, 99, 122, 123, 124, 125, 129, 130
Starnes 123
Stephens 80
Stewart 11, 37, 85, 96, 116
Stiff 26, 99
Stiltner 26, 41, 63, 68, 123, 124
Stockard 30
Stone 23
Strickland 123
Stumbo 99
Sturgell 45, 66
Sweeney 8, 36, 40, 70
Swiney 22, 26, 36, 99, 125
Sword 26
Sykes 7, 13, 19, 52, 62, 86, 99, 101, 120

T

Tackett 13, 16, 28, 59, 96, 98, 99, 123, 124
Taylor 26, 71
Thacker 57, 58, 68, 89, 91, 114, 120, 124
Thompson 21, 26, 93, 99
Thornsberry 30, 64, 106, 138
Trabue 28
True 124
Tuffs 123

V

Vance 39
Vanover 36, 67, 98
Varney 113

W

Wallace 20, 26, 38, 50, 63, 67, 82, 97, 99, 105, 107, 111, 117, 120, 122, 126, 132, 136, 140, 142

Ward 10, 18, 33, 45, 60, 67, 82, 87, 93, 98, 99, 103, 114, 132
Watson 44, 90
Webb 29, 127, 135
Weddington 26
Weigel 23, 24
West 26
Whitaker 123
Wilburn 20
Wiley 26
Wilkinson 137
Williams 17, 52, 99, 133
Williamson 61
Wright 16, 23, 26, 49, 54, 68, 83, 91, 94, 120, 122, 123, 129, 130

Y

Young 99

Loar's - Standing: Gerard Richmond, Belle Loar, Frank Loar, Harry Johns, Dockie Loar, Melvin, Layne, Joshie Peters, _____ Pendible, Layne and John Adkins. Sitting from left: unidentified, Jim Cecil, Stephen Girard Loar (standing by mother), Minerva Jones Loar and Rudolph Loar (standing by mother).

July 10, 1916, Coke Crew at Alleghany, Kentucky

Printed in the USA
CPSIA information can be obtained
at www.ICGtesting.com
JSHW060054150824
68134JS00032B/2734

9 781681 625461